How to
Sell Your
Book
Today

*Focus your book
marketing for the
new digital economy*

Karen
Hodges Miller

Open Door Publications

How to Sell Your Book Today
Book Marketing for the New Digital Economy

Copyright © 2021 by Karen Hodges Miller

ISBN: 978-1-7328202-2-7

All of the persons used as examples in this book are composites of clients the author has worked with. The names and identifying characteristics have been changed.

Published by
Open Door Publications
Willow Spring, NC 27592
www.OpenDoorPublications.com

Cover Design: Eric Labacz, www.labaczdesign.com

For my team:
Noelle, Vivian, Eric, Jennifer, and Lisa.
Thanks for all your help and support in making
Open Door Publications the best it can be.

Contents

How to Use This Book

I have stuffed a whole lot of information in this book. I know it can be intimidating, and while it is short, don't try to sit down and read it all in one sitting. It is meant to be used as a reference book you can return to over and over again.

I've used lists to give you easy-to-follow steps on many of the techniques in the book, and I also have exercises at the end of several chapters to make it easier to put these ideas into practice.

Good luck with marketing your book!

Introduction
Searching for
That Magic Marketing Bullet

Every author I know is searching for it: That Magic Marketing Bullet that will guarantee our books will become runaway best sellers. That our book will be listed in the top 10 on *The New York Times* Best Sellers list. That we will be called for interviews on national news shows. The lines of people waiting for us to sign books will wrap around the bookstore. Since this is a magic bullet, let's make sure it costs no money and takes no time or effort, too.

Since I'm an author, you know I can spin a good fantasy. And that is just what That Magic Marketing Bullet is: a fantasy. I've been searching for a long time; let me tell you, it just does not exist. There is no way to guarantee that even the best book will sell well. I've seen books I thought should be best sellers die, and I've seen others that I wondered why they sold at all hit the top of the charts.

The best sellers all have one thing in common, however. Their authors spent a lot of time and energy, and money—sometimes a lot of money, sometimes not so much—to make sure their target readers hear about their book. The only magic marketing bullet I know about is hard work.

I hear many authors, including many who are top sellers on Amazon, complain about Amazon. And I agree. There is a lot wrong with the Amazon model. Amazon is focused on making as much money as possible for Amazon, not with sharing equitably with authors. But what else do we have? Yes, there are other book distributors out there, and we will discuss "going wide" and using a lot of distributors versus targeting your sales to only one distributor. But here's the bottom line: Amazon is the best way to get your books in front of readers so you must deal with it.

Before your book even has a chance of becoming a best seller, there are certain things you must do. The list begins with writing the best, most professional book you can. I talk more about book writing in my book *Self-Publishing: You Can Do This!* I hope you'll check it out, too. While some of the material is covered in both books, this book focuses on the marketing process, specifically marketing with e-marketing techniques. Why? Because in the age of the pandemic and the new emphasis on social distancing, this type of marketing is the fastest, least expensive way to let people beyond your local circle of friends and family know you have written a book that they want and need to read. It may not be a magic bullet, but right now it is the closest thing we, as authors, have.

Chapter 1
The Rules of E-Marketing

You are a small business owner.

Today's author is a small business owner. You must learn everything you can about accounting, distribution, royalty payments and percentages, networking, and marketing—all the details the owner of any other business must learn. You must decide what you can do for yourself and when you need to hire experts to help you. The stereotype of the solitary writer starving and slaving away in the garret is just that: a stereotype, and an outdated one at that. You need a team to publish and market a book.

Writing is the easy part; it's marketing that's difficult.

Most writers have little experience with marketing—and while they may have taken classes in creative writing, been to a dozen writing conferences, and belong to a monthly writers' group, they have never marketed anything. Marketing is a skill you can learn. Start now.

Start marketing your book when you start writing.

"When do I start marketing my book?" is the first question writers ask. My answer is always the same, no matter where they are in the process: "NOW!" It is never too early to start marketing your book. You need to think about your target market, build a platform, develop a website, and start using social media as soon as you decide to write your book.

You must do your own marketing to be successful.

Best-selling authors take an active role in marketing their own work. They make appearances at book signings, develop seminars, make appearances on podcasts, and are active on social media. You are the best person to market your book. Who else has a bigger interest in making sure it is a success?

Readers are found in many places besides bookstores.

Less than half of all book sales are actually made in bookstores. Books are sold in a wide variety of retail stores, from large chain drugstores to tiny boutiques. They can be found in museums, gift shops, craft stores, and sporting goods stores. They are sold on websites, at seminars, at workshops and conferences, and at tradeshows. They are sold on Facebook and Reddit, on podcasts, and by social media influencers. Where are your readers? These days they are probably not at the bookstore. Think about where you need to look to find them.

An e-book is a must.

There was a time when writers didn't feel as if they were "real authors" unless they had a paper book to sell. These days you may be able to get by without a paper version of your book, but you must have an e-book! At the start of the pandemic in March 2020, e-book sales quickly increased 18 percent over March 2019. Store closings and shipping delays obviously increased the demand for e-books. And once readers found out how convenient they were, they have stuck with them. E-book sales have continued to be about 25 percent higher than they were before the pandemic. Even as we go back to shopping in stores, and as postal delays improve, many people will continue to stick to e-books for the convenience.

Social media is one of the best ways to let people know you are out there.

It doesn't matter whether you love Twitter, Facebook, TikTok, and Instagram or you hate them. It doesn't matter if you have never Zoomed. If you are an author with a book to sell, you need to be using social networking sites. Today social media marketing is one of the best ways to spread the news about your book. The pandemic has increased the use of social media, and even when we are able to return to in-person events, we aren't going to quit using the social media sites we have come to enjoy.

If you aren't marketing, you aren't selling.

The new rules for publishing, printing, and marketing books mean there are hundreds of thousands more books available to readers each year. How will your readers find your book in such a crowded field? If you aren't telling people about your book, they aren't going to go looking for it on their own. There is no "write it, and they will come." You have to give your potential readers a roadmap to find your book.

You need to be out there meeting people—including online if you can't meet in person.

Remember that solitary writer in the garret I mentioned in the introduction? Well, the only part of the stereotype that is true is that writer is probably starving, and definitely solitary. Most writers I know are rather shy and don't really enjoy large crowds of people. The good news: With digital marketing you can often do it from your home. With podcasts, Meetup, Zoom events, and other online ways to connect, you can now often market your book from that garret. But if you want to sell your book—I mean, actually make some money on it—you must do something to get in front of your readers and tell them about your book. This book is chock-full of ideas to help you do just that.

Chapter 2
What Is an E-Book?

What is an e-book? That may seem like a pretty simplistic question, but ask ten people what an e-book is and you'll probably get ten answers. The best answer is deceptively simple: ***An e-book is any book that can be transferred to, and read on, an electronic device.*** The format can be a PDF, a .mobi file, or an .epub file—to name the most common formats currently in use for e-books.

When e-books first entered the popular market, Amazon dominated with the Kindle. The device was strictly an e-reader and used the .mobi format. Then Barnes & Noble brought out the Nook, which used the .epub format. The decision is in, and the winner is Kindle. About 75 percent of e-books are sold for this platform.

Pros and Cons of Various Formats

Does that mean you can ignore the .epub format? It can be read on a variety of e-readers including Nook, Sony, and others, and can be purchased on a number of websites. Smashwords also uses .epub and is another option that is particularly attractive to independent authors looking for a place to sell their books other than on Amazon. Once again, there is no one right answer. There are currently several distinct advantages to focusing your e-book sales on Amazon, particularly if you are a first-time author. There can also be advantages to marketing on several different sites. We'll take a look at some of your e-book sales and marketing options throughout this book.

Using Kindle Direct Publishing (KDP) means it is possible to read books electronically on a wide variety of devices including dedicated Kindles, laptops, iPads, other tablet computers, and smartphones. The Kindle app can be downloaded to all of them with the exception of the Nook and a few other dedicated e-readers. The same is true for Nook. You can download Nook software to any device with the exception of a Kindle.

Formatting Your Book

Formatting your e-book means knowing a thing or two about how they work. E-books do not have traditional, set pages. Pages change depending on the size of the e-reader and the font size the reader chooses. As a person with poor eyesight, one of my favorite things about using an e-reader is I can increase the font to the size most comfortable for me.

E-readers also have a limited number of fonts, but some allow the reader to choose the font they prefer. The reader can also choose to increase or decrease the spacing between lines. This means readers have more choices in how a book will look than they did with traditional paper books, while the author or publisher has less choices. Most e-reader software has a nightlight setting, or the print can be changed from black-on-white to white-on-black for ease in reading under different lighting conditions.

It is essential to the creation of a professional-looking e-book to have an understanding of the e-book reading experience. The first step you should take before publishing your book as an e-book is to download the free software onto your computer, tablet, or mobile device and read a few e-books.

Next, decide if you will format the book yourself or hire a service. I know many writers prefer to do the formatting themselves, but if this is not something you want to do, you can hire an e-book formatting service to help you. Take the time to do it right, and read and check your work before you submit it. Just as with a paper book, nothing reduces your credibility and professionalism more quickly than a poorly formatted e-book.

If you have an older book that is only available to you as a paper document, you can quickly convert it to a text document using Optical Character Reader (OCR) software. Adobe Acrobat

Professional is one program that has this option. Be careful if you are using OCR software, however, because while it is a great timesaver, it is also prone to specific errors, such as confusing the letters "m," "n," and "r." I've read e-books in which certain letters always appear as capitals or in italics, or certain words are consistently misspelled. These are small but annoying errors to the reader and take some of the joy out of reading. Use the OCR software. It is excellent, but just make sure you proofread your work.

Kindle Direct Publishing makes it easy for the do-it-yourselfer. Once your paper book is formatted and proofread, with a few additional steps your Word document will be ready to upload to KDP.Amazon.com, and software on the site will convert it to an e-book.

Steps for Uploading & Converting Your Book

1. If you do not have a Contents page in your paper book, add one now, putting in only the chapter numbers and titles. Do not worry about page numbers. Remember: They don't count in an e-book. If you do have a Contents page already in your book, remove the page numbers. Add all additional content in your Contents page, such as Acknowledgments, any maps or important tables, and the About the Author page.
2. Make sure you are in "compatibility mode," which saves the document as a Word 97-2003 document.
3. Start with the Contents page. Highlight the word "Contents," click on the "Insert" tab, then click on "Bookmark." In the dialogue box type "ref_TOC" and click "Add." Go to each chapter page, highlight the chapter title, click on "Bookmark," and type in the chapter. *You cannot use any spaces.* I suggest you use an abbreviation such as CH1, CH2, etc. Go through the entire book, and do this for all chapters and any other content you want the reader to easily locate.
4. Now you are ready to create your links. Go back to the Contents page and hyperlink it to each individual chapter page. To do this, highlight the chapter title on the Contents page. On the "Insert" tab, open the dialogue box marked "Link." On the left, click on the "Place in This Document"

box. This brings up the bookmarks you just created. Select the bookmark that corresponds to the highlighted chapter, then click "OK." The link should turn blue and be underlined if you have done it correctly.

5. Next, link the chapters back to the Contents page so that readers can click back and forth if they wish. Go back to each chapter page and hyperlink back to "ref_TOC."

6. Always check a few of your links to make sure they are working.

7. Go through your document and make sure any references you have to websites or email addresses are also linked. This is easy. Just type the Uniform Resource Locator (URL), hit one space, and the link should be active.

Now you are ready to upload your book to Amazon. The steps for other e-reader sales sites, such as Nook and Smashwords, are similar. However, some sites, such as Smashwords, require that you have your book already formatted as an .epub document.

There is conversion software available that will convert a Word document or PDF to an .epub or .mobi file. I have tried several and prefer Calibre (www.calibre-ebook.com). Do some research before you decide which software you prefer. Many have a trial period so you can try them out before you buy.

Pricing Your E-Book

Pricing for e-books is as varied as it is for paper books. If you are writing a technical, medical, legal, or financial book, you can charge more than if you are writing a "trade" or mass market book.

For most fiction and nonfiction books from new authors, I suggest starting at $3.99. It is easier to change the price of e-books, and later on I will explain free and reduced price e-book promotions. To launch a book, however, $3.99 is the current "sweet spot."

Make sure, no matter who your publisher is, that you have control of your e-book pricing and promotions.

Should All Books Be E-Books?

As e-readers become more popular, and technology improves, the list of books that should not be formatted as e-books is growing shorter. Readers are more likely to purchase fiction than nonfiction as an e-book, but some nonfiction does quite well electronically. Technology and computer books are obvious choices for e-books. Business books also do well.

Interestingly, while women were the first to adopt e-readers, today the largest demographic is men age 35 to 54 years. Now that color has come to e-readers, children's picture books are becoming more popular. Since the pandemic, many schools are distributing tablet computers for homework, research, and reading.

I have recently worked with books that require more complicated formatting and links to audio and video. They are beautiful, but only do well on iPads and certain higher end e-book readers. They do not work as well on cellphones or older, more simplified readers. Do not try to format these types of books yourself. You do need an expert to make everything work smoothly.

Reading books on tablets, computers, and smartphones allows for increasing interactivity. E-readers include search, bookmark, and note-taking features. Links allow the reader to jump to specific chapters. Plus the back-of-the-book author bio now routinely includes a direct link to the author's website and a request for reviews.

There are still, however, books that should not be published as e-books. If you are writing a workbook or journal, an e-book will only work if you do some rewriting and reformatting, taking out the original journaling pages or question-and-answer sections and changing the book to state something such as "on a separate sheet of paper write...."

An author I know recently uploaded a workbook to Amazon KDP. She spent a lot of money to get it formatted as an e-book because it included many charts, graphs, and workbook sections with lines where the reader was to write. After only a few months, Amazon insisted that she take the e-book down. In fact, Amazon made it clear that not removing it could result in penalties. Here is a portion of their email to the author.

"If you wish to make this book available for sale on Amazon, please resubmit it with content that complies with our guidelines. Note that books meant to be filled in by the user (e.g., journals, coloring books) can be published through KDP as paperback books. As a reminder, since publishing books that require resources beyond a Kindle device or Kindle application (Phone/Mac/PC) is against our guidelines, we may suspend or terminate accounts that repeatedly try to do so."

If Amazon threatens to suspend your account, take down the book. It is not worth the risk, especially if you have several books already selling on Amazon.

As you make your decision on paper book, e-book, or both, look again at your target reader and your marketing plan. The age of the reader, the type of book you are writing, and the type of marketing you plan to do should all be part of your decision.

Some Final Thoughts

E-books are covered under the exact same intellectual property laws as paper books. Make sure you always copyright your work, no matter what format you publish it in.

You want to be paid for the e-books you sell on the various websites where they are listed. Each site has slightly different registration rules. You will need to enter your banking information for Electronic Funds Transfer (EFT). Read the directions and rules carefully on each site, and follow them scrupulously, then keep track of your sales and your bank transfers.

Exercise 1
E-Book Exploration

Follow these steps to learn more about e-books.

1. Download both the free Nook and Kindle software to a mobile device.
2. Read at least one book on each device to get an idea of how books look and feel as an e-book.
3. Play with the settings on the e-reader. See how different settings will change the experience for the reader.

Chapter 3
Marketing Basics

You've done it! Finally, after months or even years spent writing and editing your book, finding a publisher, choosing a cover design, debating over type fonts, suffering through proofreading and corrections, and dealing with all the usual setbacks and delays of a complex project, you have your book in hand. It is beautiful. It is your baby. You want everyone in the world to read it, and you're sure that as soon as a couple of book reviewers find it, you'll head straight to the top of the best seller charts.

Unless you market your book wisely, however, only your mother and a few of your friends and colleagues will buy a copy. ***Do you know how many copies the average book sells? Between 200 and 500.*** That statistic includes every author from internationally famous ones, such as Stephen King and J.K. Rowling, to the John Doe who sells 15 copies of his book on the history of postage stamps to his philatelist club.

So how do you help your book rise above the pack and get noticed when millions of individual book titles are published in the United States each year?

Your Purpose

The first step in deciding how to market your book is to look at your purpose in writing it. Yes, I know, you are thinking "of course, my purpose is to sell as many books as possible." But is it really? Unless you are clear on why you are doing something, how will you know if you have achieved the results you are looking for? Your purpose in writing your book will be a driving force in how you market it; whether you write fiction or nonfiction, you may have any number of purposes in writing it.

A fiction writer may hope to sell enough books to make a full-time career in writing. Or she might want to use her book to gain credibility in the literary world and be asked to lead writers' conferences and workshops, become a guest lecturer at a school, or be offered a permanent post as a professor in a university English department.

For nonfiction writers the purpose can be even more varied. Many authors hope to use their book to develop a national platform for their ideas. Others might see their book as only one of many items they will sell on their website to build their brand or increase their profits. Still others see their books as strictly a way to enhance their credibility with prospective clients. What are you trying to achieve with your book? Think about the answer before you even start to think about the various ways to market it.

10 Things to Remember

What are the most important things to remember when marketing? They are as wide-ranging as the number of marketing experts you ask, but these are some basic points I like to keep in mind while marketing my own books and those of other authors.

Marketing a book is marketing *you*.
You are selling your expertise, your knowledge, and your ability to tell a story and to engage your audience. You aren't just selling your book; you are selling yourself.

The day you stop marketing your book is the day it stops selling.
If you don't tell people about your book, they won't go looking for it on their own. There is no "write it, and they will come." You have to give your potential readers a roadmap to find it.

Selling to everyone is selling to no one.
Your target market is your "sweet spot," the 80 percent of the market most likely to purchase your book. Yes, your book may appeal to a wide variety of people, but which group is the most likely to buy your book? What traits do they share? Where will you find them? How can you let them know that your book is available for sale?

Don't be a miser; give your books away.
I recently read an interesting statistic. One book given away can encourage 10 book sales. This is a very important point to remember. Authors get very cost-conscious with their books; they are afraid to give away that sample copy. Sow your books like seeds on the wind—you never know what fruit they will bring. This goes for e-books as much as for paper books. A free giveaway, properly handled, can boost your Amazon rankings and result in more "pages read" over the next several weeks—for which you do get paid.

Depend on yourself; no one cares about your book like you do.
YOU are the person who cares the most about your product. YOU are the person who ultimately must make the decisions about which marketing techniques to use. If it doesn't feel right, don't do it.

Hire experts to help you.
This seems to be the opposite advice of "Depend on yourself" above, but it is not. Yes, you are the person who cares the most about your product, and you should make the final decisions. But you also cannot do it all or be an expert in everything. Hire the experts you need in public relations, marketing, and social media. Spending your money wisely will bring returns in sales and recognition for you and your book.

There is no overnight success.
The media love to tout the overnight success story, but if you really look hard, you'll find years of study and hard work

went into most so-called overnight success stories.

Don't give up.

Pick a marketing technique and try it for several months. If it doesn't work, try another technique, and then another. Don't just try one marketing technique and, if it doesn't bring you the results you want, give up. I've known too many authors who do this, then say to themselves, "Well, that didn't work. I guess no one wants to buy my book." Instead of giving up on your book, find a new way to market it.

Don't try to do it all at once.

Here is a corollary to "Don't give up" above: There are hundreds of different marketing techniques you can use—don't try to do them all at once unless you have a large publicity staff behind you. Do some research, pick three or four things you think will work best for you and your book, and do them well.

Always look professional.

This goes for both you and your book. You wouldn't go to a business event wearing torn jeans and a t-shirt. Why would you try to save money by skipping steps on your book's appearance? Pay for a professional editor, proofreader, and graphic artist. Make sure your book looks as professional as you do.

Exercise 2
Finding Your Purpose

On a separate sheet of paper answer these questions:

1. What do you want your book to do for you?
2. What do you want your book to do for others?
3. Who are your readers? Write a detailed description of the person you think will read your book.
   a. What is their age?
   b. What is their gender?
   c. What is their profession?
   d. What do they do in their spare time?
   e. Where do they hang out on social media?

Chapter 4
Your Marketing Plan

Before you can effectively market your book, you need a plan. Without one, your marketing will feel helter-skelter, and probably bring you very few positive results. Start by thinking creatively about how to market your book using both digital and in-person marketing. Everything from tweeting and blogging to good old-fashioned networking should be considered. One author I know recently sold 200 books in the first 10 days after publication using only word of mouth marketing and networking in her community. With a good plan you can do this, and more, too.

Here is a sample marketing plan to get you started. Use a separate sheet of paper to write down the suggestions that you think will work for you, and add additional ideas of your own.

General Strategies

These strategies don't necessarily focus on e-marketing but are tried and true marketing techniques all authors should consider.

1. Send news releases to local, regional, and national publications about your book.
2. Send copies of your book to book review websites.
3. Have a party. Invite your friends, family, and business associates, and announce it to the press, too.
4. Develop add-on products that sell your book. If you're a fiction writer, for instance, can your book be adapted for a computer game? Can you sell t-shirts, jewelry, mugs, etc.?

5. These days most books are not sold in traditional bookstores. Make a list of gift shops and boutiques selling items related to your book.

E-Marketing Strategies

These techniques focus on e-marketing. Don't worry if you don't yet know what they are. We will discuss them in the next chapters.

1. Kindle countdown deal.
2. E-book promotion sites.
3. Use Facebook and other social media sites to tell friends and followers about your book.
4. Place a book trailer on YouTube and other internet sites to advertise your book.
5. Blog and tweet about your area of expertise.

Now, using these ideas, create your own marketing plan. You don't have to do them all—pick a few that are right for you and your book. At the end of the chapter is an exercise to help you create your own plan.

Create a Budget

Once you've decided on how to market your book, ask yourself which portions of your plan you can do yourself and which will need the help of a book publicist, marketer, or social media expert. Sure, you can probably write a news release that will get you into the local paper, but if your goal is to get an interview on a national news show, you will need help getting there. You may be active with YouTube, but can you create your own, professional-looking book trailer?

No one starts out with an interview in *The Wall Street Journal* or on a national talk show. Get your feet wet with local marketing, then regional marketing, then go for the national audience.

Set up a timeline and a budget, and be realistic about it. Marketing costs money, but it can pay for itself in increased sales of your book and increased recognition of you as an expert in your field.

Pandemic Sales Trends

Some new trends in book buying have emerged since the pandemic began that authors and readers should know. The following statistics come from Ingram Content Group, the largest book distributor in the world.

1. Books, music, and videos saw some of the largest increases in online sales of any category of products.
2. In May 2020 book, music, and video sales increased 62 percent over May 2019.
3. In 2020 book sales were the highest they have been in 15 years with 627 million units sold.
4. This 627 million units sold includes 133 million e-books.
5. While paper books still sell significantly more units than e-books, e-book sales grew by approximately 45 million units.

The most significant finding is that 48 percent of shoppers say they will continue to buy online after the pandemic and social distancing have ended. This finding means that the pandemic marketing strategies you learn now will continue to be valuable for years to come.

Exercise 3
Sample Marketing Plan

Here's a sample marketing activity for you to study. Use this as a guide to create your own marketing plan.

Marketing Activity:
Send out books to 10 Instagram Book Bloggers. (Instagram bloggers usually prefer a paper copy of the book so they can add photos to their reviews.)
Purpose:
To spread the word about the book; it can also increase internet mentions of the book and improve search engine optimization (SEO).
Steps:
1. Search on the internet for bloggers who write about books in your genre. Look for the most popular bloggers with the largest following.
2. Carefully check the bloggers' guidelines and follow them. Send an email asking if they are interested in reviewing your book.
3. Once you have an affirmative reply, promptly send the book along with any other information they request such as a bio or a jpeg of yourself.

Budget:
1. $45.00 ($3.50 author cost for your book plus shipping to you from your printer/distributor)
2. $10.00 for padded envelopes to mail books
3. $15.00 for book rate postage to mail books
Follow-Up: Check with bloggers one week after mailing to confirm they have received their books.

Chapter 5
Prepublication Marketing

You need to begin marketing your book even before you finish writing it. In fact, you should begin to develop your marketing strategy to sell your book at the same time you begin working on the outline for writing it.

Learn a lesson from filmmakers, who are great at building an audience long before the film's release date. You need to do the same for your book. Start with the people you know, then move out from there, which means you need to start with word-of-mouth marketing—and in this case I mean that literally. Tell people about your book. Tell your family, tell your friends, tell your coworkers, tell strangers you meet at a party or networking event. It is amazing what the phrase, "I'm writing a book on…" can do.

A fellow author who was working on her second book before COVID-19 describes the magic this phrase carries with it.

"When I was writing my first book, I never told anyone about it until it was almost ready to be published," she says. "This time I'm only on Chapter 3, but I was at a networking lunch the other day, and when it was time to introduce myself, I said I was writing a book and mentioned the title. Two people came up to me later and set up meetings with me. They said they really identified with the title of the book, and since I was writing about the subject, I must be an expert."

As soon as I started writing my first book, I also experienced something similar. I mentioned I was writing a book about how to write a book. It turned out that the person I was speaking to was the program chairman for another organization, and always on the lookout for guest speakers. Suddenly, I was making the rounds of several chapters of a statewide organization.

Fast-forward to the pandemic or postpandemic world. You can still network; but now you will be doing it via Zoom.

Make a list of the organizations you belong to. Are they meeting online? Even if you haven't attended a virtual meeting of the group since the pandemic started, find out what time the next meeting is, and on what platform. Show up, participate, and talk about your book!

There is a new advantage to all of these Zoom meetings. You can now network with people in multiple cities or states in the same day! If you belong to a national organization, "visit" several of its local chapters—no matter what state they are in.

Word of mouth is awesome. You never know who you are speaking with or who they know. So get over your shyness, your modesty, or your fear, and tell the world about your book.

Another quick way to tell people about your book is to add it to your email signature.

For example:

John Smith

Author of *The ABCs of Growing Cabbages*,

available soon

Keep the date of publication vague at first, then make it more definite as you go along. The phrase can change from "available soon" to "coming this fall" to "on sale October 20" and finally to a link to your website's shopping cart.

Your Back Cover "Blurb"

Before you can really talk about your book, you have to know what it is about. Now is the time to create a two- or three-paragraph description for your book. You will use it on the back cover of the printed copy, on your Amazon sales page, on other book sales sites, when you create e-book promotions, in press releases—the list goes on and on.

I've seen short blurbs and long ones. I've had people tell me to never start or end with a question, and people who say to always use questions. You get the idea. Here are a few pointers:

✓ You are writing a marketing piece, not a book report. Catch the reader's attention in the first sentence, and give them a compelling reason to buy your book.

✓ Think "benefits," not "features." If you have ever worked in a sales position, you have heard this phrase. What is the difference? A feature is something the product has. A benefit is how that feature helps the buyer.

For example, if you are selling a refrigerator, the phrase "it has seven different food drawers" would be a feature, whereas saying, "the seven different drawers make it easy for you to keep different types of food at different temperatures, keeping them fresher longer," is taking that feature and turning it into a benefit for the customer.

The same is true for your book. What are the benefits for the reader? It may be easy to figure this out if you are writing nonfiction; for fiction writers, it is often more difficult. Think of your "benefits" as why the reader wants to read your book. Make your cover copy so compelling the reader needs to know how the book ends.

Here are some pointers for writing a book description that sells:

• Begin with a headline of about 200 characters. Bold the headline so it stands out. The headline can ask a question, describe a major theme of the book, and make the reader want to know more.

• The body of your description should be two to three paragraphs long. It should entice the reader to buy the book. Give the reader some information on theme, plot (no, you don't have to do a spoiler; instead, it should be a teaser), and what they will learn if it is a nonfiction book.

• End with a short paragraph emphasizing value, the intended audience, and why they need to buy this book now.

Social Networking

If you haven't started social networking, do so today. If you have a Facebook page, start posting about your book. Give your friends status updates on how many chapters you have written.

Talk about the writing process, post excerpts, add a link to a pre-order page, and announce your book launch party and other events. These are your friends, after all, and they are on your page because they are interested in what you are doing.

Are you on LinkedIn, Google Plus, ZoomInfo, or other similar sites? If not, you should be. Pick one or two, and join now. However, even if you haven't signed up for some of these sites, you may be listed there. Search your name on several sites, and see if you are listed and if the information is accurate.

It's particularly important if you have a common name. I recently checked one of these profile sites and found my information was mixed with a high school music teacher in the Midwest with a similar name. Most of these sites allow you to log in and edit your own information without paying a fee. Make sure when you are looking over your information you add your book, and, if possible, a link to a website where it can be purchased.

Blogs and Newsletters

A blog gives you the space to post longer excerpts from your book, and it can also increase your credibility and your name recognition. Start your blog while you are still writing your book; it takes time to develop a following and prospective buyers for your book. Send people to your blog by linking it to Facebook or other social media.

You may also want to start a newsletter, which is a little more complex because you must get permission from the people to whom you send your newsletter. You don't want to be a spammer. But getting their permission is simpler than it seems.

I suggest Mailchimp as a great service to use for your email newsletter. It is free. It does take a little bit of learning to use, but there are tutorials. Following its permission process will help keep you from accidentally spamming friends, acquaintances, and readers.

Start your newsletter list by going through your email contacts and adding their names to the list. Collect business cards at networking events. If you have a booth at a book festival, put out a piece of paper to collect emails. Your first newsletter may only have 10 or 12 people on it, but you've got to start somewhere.

Other Prepublication Marketing

As a writer in the 21st century, you are a small business owner. You need to delegate the tasks you don't do well and focus on the tasks that only you can do and where you have expertise.

Too many authors I know—and I'll include myself in this list—market their books haphazardly. They start a blog, write for a few weeks, then lose interest and quit writing. They send a press release to five or 10 media outlets without learning who they should contact or doing any follow-up. Then they get discouraged when they get no response from the media. They are asked to do a workshop by a local organization and get great feedback, but never send out requests to speak to other organizations—and then wonder why they never get another request to speak.

Do any of these scenarios sound like you? Get out of the rut this kind of "start and stop" marketing has put you in, and develop a marketing plan for both you and your book.

Get Some Professional Photos Made

One thing I hear the most groans about from authors is getting a professional photograph made. I admit I've moaned, groaned, and put this off as much as possible myself. The fact remains you need at least one, well-done professional photograph of yourself.

Spend the money, and get some good photographs made. Don't use COVID-19 as an excuse. Photographers have had to become more creative about how to continue to make money while social distancing. Outdoor photos, porch photos, and other out-of-the-studio sites can make interesting author photos. Definitely get one great head shot for your press kit.

Do NOT stand in front of a wall and have a friend or relative take your photo with a cellphone. You don't want to look as if you are in a police lineup. Do not use candid photos either. Most are blurry and don't reproduce very well.

Put Together a Media Kit

Put together a press kit that can be obtained three ways: Hard copy mailed out to the media, sent by email as a combination of

PDFs and JPEG files, and also downloaded from your website. When mailing a press kit use excellent quality paper and, along with a hard copy version of your photo, add a link to a website where it can be downloaded as a .jpeg file so that it can be easily used digitally. The goal of a press kit is to make it as easy as possible for anyone in the media to write about you and your book.

Your media kit should contain:

1. A basic press release announcing the book, which can be adapted for seminars, special appearances, podcasts, book launches, etc.
2. Your photo and a link for downloading the .jpeg files
3. Your bio—make it one page or less
4. A photo or .jpeg file of your book cover
5. An excerpt from your book—no more than a few pages, please
6. Promotional materials, such as postcards or bookmarks

Promotional Materials

Expect a two- to three-month period from when you have a completed manuscript and a beautiful cover, and you'll be waiting for proofreading, printing proofs, and finally—your book. This is when you want to really start marketing your new product. Have your graphic designer make a bookmark, business card, or postcard to match the cover. It should include the title of the book, the publication date, your name and contact information, and a web address for preordering the book. Hand these materials out instead of your regular business card. While I've seen both business cards and postcards used successfully this way, my favorite marketing tool for books is a bookmark. After all, what could be more appropriate? I've also found while people are inclined to quickly discard postcards and business cards, they are more likely to keep and use bookmarks.

What Help Do You Need?

Just as with producing a book, most of us don't have the time, skills, or contacts to completely handle all of the marketing for our book or our business.

Once you have developed your marketing plan, look at each of the elements in it. What can you do yourself, and what should you hire out to other professionals?

For instance, you may want to do your own social networking but have no idea how to write a press release. There are plenty of good marketing and communications companies in every community who have the experience, the contacts, and the expertise to help you. It will take you several hours, or more likely days, to develop your own media list. A marketing company already has that information at its fingertips—and its lists are usually larger and more up-to-date than ones you can develop on your own. It may be more effective to ask a marketing company or public relations agency to handle this portion of your marketing.

Working With the Media

Start to research your local media before you are ready to launch your book. I can't tell you the number of people who have complained to me over the years that their local newspaper, television, or radio station pays no attention to them. When I question them on how they contacted the media, however, I often find they have either made one or two half-hearted attempts and given up or have blanketed every outlet they could think of with a press release that was so general it gave no information.

Remember this marketing rule: If you are targeting everyone, you are targeting no one. This is as true for marketing to the media as it is to marketing to readers.

The first thing to remember about the media is that it is not one, amorphous blob. Each separate newspaper, magazine, television, radio station, and podcast has its own special niche audience and its own special way of targeting that niche. This is also true for online reviewers and other online news outlets.

Let's take a look at that broad category called "women's magazines." While, yes, they all target women, they are not identical. *Self, Redbook, Good Housekeeping, InStyle, Parents,* and *Cosmopolitan* are all magazines aimed at women, but their focuses are not identical. You would not promote a book on child care to *Cosmopolitan,* but you would promote it to both *Redbook* and *Parents* magazine. I could continue with my examples, but I hope you get the point. So here are some for working with the media.

They are relevant whether you are trying to get an article in your local weekly newspaper or setting up podcast or national television interviews.

Once you have a list of media outlets that look like a good fit for you, find the right person to contact at each one. Even smaller news outlets have a variety of editors or reporters who deal with specific topics. Find out who deals with your topic. If you are planning a book event, it may be a different person than a general press release about your book. The same is true for contacting television shows. Do not address the press release to the host of the show. The show's producer is the person who most often chooses the guests.

Podcasts and blog book reviews are a very important part of book marketing. Do not forget about them in your search for the right media outlet. If they have the right target market, you may get more direct benefit in greater sales than by being on a regional or national show with a larger, but less targeted, audience.

When people ask me the best way to get an article in the newspaper, I tell them, "Get to know an editor or reporter." The same advice holds true for all media.

Don't just send out a press release and expect it to be used. Whenever you send out a press release, make sure that you follow up. I recently spoke with someone who had followed up his emailed press releases by mailing out cards with a photo of his product. He wondered why he hadn't received any response. Mailing information is not the same as speaking to someone.

Follow-up means a personal phone call. Be polite, inquire if the reporter got the press release, and ask if you can give the reporter any additional information.

Your Website

If you don't have a website, you need one. If you do have a website, you need to add a page about your book on it. You may decide to add a shopping cart feature so customers can buy your book directly from you, or you may choose to simply link your book page to selling sites such as Amazon. In any case, you will need to spend some money on your website, which can be anywhere from a few hundred dollars to several thousand dollars—

depending on whether or not you already have a website and how elaborate you want it to be.

If you've never had a website before, shop around and talk to several different web designers. Each one will have different ideas, techniques, and prices for websites.

If you are planning to develop a separate website for your book, purchase the URL and develop the site before you publish the book. This action is important because you can start developing traffic to your site, make announcements about your book's availability, and create a home for your blog.

You may want to use the title of the book as your URL or purchase a website in your own name if you plan to write several books. A one- to three-page website is perfectly fine for an author site. The home page should advertise the book, give the date of publication, showcase the book cover, and provide links to any other websites you have. Your home page should also prominently display a link to allow people to preorder your book (which will become a link to an Amazon or other bookseller site as soon as it becomes available). The third page can contain your bio and links to a downloadable press kit. Your contact information—email and phone number—should be easily found on all of the pages of your website.

Exercise 4
Prepublication Plan

I've given you a lot of information in this last chapter. Here it is broken into an easy checklist for you to follow. You may not want to do everything on this list. Write down the steps you plan to take, then keep of record of what you have done so you can keep track of your marketing efforts.

1. Tell people about your book.
2. Look for organizations you can "visit" via Zoom meetings if you cannot visit in person.
3. Add your "coming soon" announcement to your email signature; update it as needed.
4. Develop your back cover blurb to help you tell people about your book.
5. Choose three social media sites to become active on. Start to post regularly, making sure to mention your book.
6. Begin collecting and saving email addresses of friends, family, coworkers, and other associates.
7. Start to regularly blog or send out an email newsletter.
8. Get professional photos made.
9. Put together a media kit.
10. Prepare and order promotional materials.
11. Make a list of media you want to send media kits to. Check their publication deadlines, and keep notes on them.
12. If you don't have a website, develop one now; if you do have one, add your book information to it.

Chapter 6
The 100 Review Book Launch

How will you launch your book? You might have always dreamed of a book signing at a public library or a great party for friends and family. But we just aren't sure when that will be realistic again. What happens with public events is up in the air right now—and may be for some time to come. It takes several months to plan a large public event so when we don't know what the social distancing rules will be, it makes it difficult to put the money and effort into planning something elaborate.

This doesn't mean you can't plan a great book launch, however. It just means that today's book launches look different than those of the past.

Even if your book launch will be totally digital—especially if your book launch will be totally digital—the time to start planning your launch is several months before your book's date of publication.

Why 100 Reviews?

Why am I emphasizing reviews instead of sales? Because new times call for new techniques. These days most books are bought online, not in bookstores. As potential readers browse Amazon for books, one of the first things they do before buying is to check a product's reviews. Research shows that 90 percent of internet shoppers read online reviews, and 84 percent trust those online reviews as much as they trust a personal recommendation.

Reviews lead to sales—and the reverse is also true. A lack of reviews turns off potential readers and keeps them from buying.

The 100 Review Book Launch is a very simple technique that anyone can follow. It is not complex. It does not take a lot of money. What it does take is time, planning, and, most importantly, a willingness to put yourself out there and tell friends, family, and acquaintances that you have written a book—and that to make it successful, you need their help.

Before You Begin

Whether you are planning to use the 100 Review Book Launch or have another type of book launch planned, it is important to first understand a few things about the way Amazon works for authors.

✓ Amazon KDP allows an author to set a preorder date up to one year before the e-book goes on sale. While I don't suggest you set your preorder this far ahead, do set it up a minimum of six weeks before you plan your launch.

✓ Preorders cannot be set up for paper books, only for e-books. :

✓ Preorders contribute toward sales rank for your book even before it is released, which means a book with a large number of preorders will have greater searchability when potential readers type in keywords. This action, in turn, helps more potential readers find your book.

✓ E-book preorders can be set worldwide so that you can tap potential readers throughout the world.

You set up your preorder for your e-book just as you would for a book you are releasing immediately. The only difference is that you will set an advance date. You can find out more about how to set up your book on Amazon in Chapter 9.

The detail page will look exactly like the detail page for a book that is already on sale. To complete the preorder you must have at least one page to upload. I recommend just uploading a one-page Word document that says: "Preorder page for *Title of the Book*."

You have until 72 hours before your book goes on sale to upload your final manuscript, but I suggest you plan to upload any final changes at least a week before that date to give you time to iron out any problems. Place a note on your calendar to check on your KDP listing one week before the launch date so you don't forget. You really don't want your family, friends, and fans to upload that "sample" sheet instead of the book they are anxiously waiting to see. Even if you are sure that you have uploaded everything correctly, go in and check in again. You made that preorder listing quite a long time ago so double-check it.

Amazon does enforce penalties to keep authors from abusing the preorder guidelines. If you cancel a preorder, you will not be able to set up another preorder for any other e-book for one year.

Decide on your book's price when you set up your preorder, and stick to it. If you decide to lower the price before the preorder is over, Amazon will refund the difference to any customers who have already ordered the book.

You can enroll your book in the KDP Select program. We'll explain KDP Select in Chapter 8.

The Plan

Now that you know some of the basics of working with Amazon preorders, here is the plan for the 100 Review Book Launch.

- Six weeks before your book is scheduled to launch, make a list of 100 people you know and have an email address for. These can be family, friends, clients, and fans. Anyone you know well enough to ask for help. If you don't have an email for someone you really want on your list, call them and ask for it.
- Five weeks before your launch, make sure you have a proofread, print-ready PDF of your e-book, with the cover, ready to email to reviewers. Now is also the time to set up your Amazon e-book preorder.
- Do NOT set up your paper book at this time. As soon as you approve your paper book in KDP, it will appear for sale on Amazon. This can negate the effect of the e-book launch.

- As soon as your preorder is live on Amazon, send a personal, individual email to each person on your list. Do NOT use an email newsletter, blind copy, or any other method of sending out group emails. The goal is to create a very personal request to each person on your list. Explain in the letter that you are writing a book. Give a short, one- or two-sentence summary of it, and ask if you can send the person a free PDF of the book before the launch in exchange for a promise to write a review of the book *and post it on the day of your book launch.* The letter should make it clear you are looking for an honest review. If readers don't think the book is worth five stars, they should not feel forced to give you a five-star review.
- Set up a spread sheet to record the responses you receive. Make sure you immediately send the PDF along with a thank you email to anyone who agrees to review your book.
- Touch base with the people on your list both at three weeks and at two weeks prior to your launch. For the people who have agreed to read the book, remind them about the review date. For the people who have not responded to your request, ask them again if they would like to review the book. Make sure you keep a record of anyone who has specifically said they are not interested in writing a review, and don't bother them again. Some people just are not comfortable with writing reviews.
- One day before your book goes live on Amazon, send everyone on the list who has agreed to read the book a final reminder to post their review on Amazon the next day.
- Follow up the day after with personal thank-you notes to the people who have reviewed your book and additional requests for a review from those who have promised them. Continue to follow up in the coming weeks.

Not everyone who has received an early PDF will respond with a review. And not all of them will be a five-star review. But if you follow this plan diligently, you should receive 100 reviews within six to eight weeks.

Exercise 5
Sample First Email for Book Review Plan

Hi _____

Over the last year I've been writing a book titled *Book title here in italics*. It is about [add one-sentence description here].

In just five weeks it will be available on Amazon.

You may not be aware of how important reviews are in making sure a book in successful on Amazon. It increases the credibility of the author and the searchability of the book.

I need your help with this.

May I send you a free PDF of my book for you to look at now, before its publication? All I ask is that you skim through it or read a few chapters in the next five weeks and leave a review with your honest feedback and thoughts on [date], the day my book launches.

Please let me know if you can help me with this and if you have any questions.

Thank you so much for your help!

For second and third letters just adjust the wording as needed, and don't forget to send a thank-you note to everyone who uploads a review.

Chapter 7
But Wait, There's More

You didn't think it would be that easy, did you? Contacting your first 100 readers is only the start of your book launch. We've only given away your book so far. Now we want to work on selling it. This next step helps you tell more potential readers—people you already know—about your book.

Again, you need to start with a list, a larger one this time. Do you already have an email newsletter? A list of clients? Contacts on your Facebook, LinkedIn, or other social media? Many people will say they don't have a list. If you are one of those people, I want you to stop and think about all the people you come in contact with. You might not have an email address for them; now is the time to ask for it. No matter how small your potential list is right now, get started on it. Think creatively.

Dealing With Objections—Yours and Others

We will pause here to take a moment to deal with the objections I know many of you are having right now. How do I know this? Because I used to make these objections, too.

1. I can't do that.
2. I don't know anyone.
3. I don't have time.
4. I don't want to bother anyone.
5. If my book is good, people will just find it.
6. It doesn't look right to market my own book; it's like blowing my own horn.

Yes, you can do this. It isn't hard. You know a lot of people; you have just never stopped to make a list of them. Now is the time to do that, which brings me to objection number three: "I don't have time." If you want to sell your book, you have to make the time.

That brings us to the last three objections, which are really about lack of confidence in yourself and your work. I know it is hard to put yourself out there. Your work is very personal. You have spent hours, maybe years, on it, and you are afraid people won't like it.

Guess what? Some of them won't. But many of them will.

So many people, women in particular, are afraid to tell people about their own accomplishments. We hear our parents' and teachers' voices whispering in the background, "Don't brag about yourself. It's rude."

To market your book you have to shut down all of those insidious whispers and forget what you learned in kindergarten.

If you don't tell people about your book, no one else will! If you don't ask for what you need, people will never know you need it.

Stop for a moment, take a deep breath, and say to yourself, "My book is good. It will help people."

Now back to our regularly scheduled program!

The Special Offer Book Launch Plan

Create a special offer in which you will give away a free PDF with useful information that your potential reader would like to know. This approach can be easier for a nonfiction writer, particularly if you already have a business, but fiction writers can do this as well.

What should be in this PDF? Special sales or learning tips for a business coach. A short story for a fiction writer. A prayer for an inspirational writer. If what you are planning to offer is one page, you can use some fancy fonts and clip art to create a poster that can be hung on the wall. Just make sure what you are offering has some value to the reader and makes sense with your brand and your genre.

Now that you have decided on your free giveaway, use that list you have created to make your offer. Since you want to put this offer out to more people than you did with the 100 Review Book Launch, now is the time to use an email newsletter. You can also post it on LinkedIn, Facebook, and other social media.

Ask your people to:

1. Preorder your book. Always add a link to the preorder page in everything you send out. Make it as easy as possible for people to find and purchase your book.
2. Once the person has ordered the book, ask them to take a screen print of the email receipt for the preorder and send it to you.
3. In exchange for the proof of their purchase of the book, send them your special PDF.
4. Be sure to send out the PDF right away. You've asked them to do something for you. Your free PDF, along with a thank-you note, should be sent as quickly as possible.
5. At the end of the free offer—on the PDF if it is applicable, or in the email—ask for a review, and give the link to your book again to make it easy for them.
6. Make it clear whenever you make this offer that you are happy for your readers to pass the offer on to others. This is word-of-mouth marketing. You want to get the buzz going about your book.

This type of marketing plan has several advantages:

1. It will help you to increase sales on the first day your book is launched.
2. It will increase your database of potential readers, fans, and clients by giving you more email addresses to add to your database.
3. By asking for reviews from people who are already familiar with you and your work, you increase the likelihood of favorable reviews.

While both the 100 Review Book Launch and the Special

Offer Book Launch plans are designed specifically to be used soon after your book is released, they can also be used throughout the life of your book to breathe new life into a product whose sales are flagging.

Other Book Launch Tips and Techniques

Don't forget about using the media to help you get the word out about your book. These days "the media" does not just mean newspapers, radio, and television. It includes podcasts, bloggers, and social media influencers—anyone who has an audience you would like to tap into to sell your book.

These outlets need anywhere from a few weeks to a few months to schedule articles and interviews. Podcasts are one of the most important ways to get the word out about a new book these days, and don't count out those local newspapers and radio stations. The deadlines for each of these types of media are fairly short. Magazines, however, plan their production schedules from three to six months ahead. Find out the deadlines for the particular media resource you want to attract, and send announcements out accordingly.

In-Person Book Launches

While this book is mostly focused on digital ways to market your book, we should also talk about good old-fashioned, in-person marketing. Prior to the pandemic, parties were a fun and exciting way to launch a book to local friends and fans. The downside is a party can cost a lot of money.

If you do decide on hosting an in-person book launch, here are a few tips.

1. Consider partnering with a local business to host the launch. For example, if you are writing a book on hiking, ask a local sporting goods store to host your book launch. Likewise, a gift boutique would be a good partner for any book aimed at a female audience.
2. You can also contact local bookstores to see if they will partner with you for a book signing. Make sure—no matter what type of business you partner with—that the arrangements about book sales are very clear. Who will supply the books?

What percentage of profits will each of you get from book sales made during the signing?

I've seen all types of arrangements and agreements made between authors and local businesses; the secret is to have a very specific, written agreement made beforehand. These types of events don't just have to be used during the first few weeks after your book is printed. Book events are a very effective way to gain new readers throughout the life of your book, and they are particularly excellent at bringing in new sales for book one right after you publish book two.

Where Can People Buy Your Book?

While I want you to limit your e-book to Amazon to take advantage of the KDP Select royalties, your paper book may be listed on a number of sites. If you have used Ingram Spark to print your book, it will automatically be listed on various bookselling websites such as BarnesandNoble.com, BooksaMillion.com, and Google Books, as well as Amazon.com

Google your book title and International Standard Book Number (ISBN) to see where it is listed. It may show up in some unexpected places. Check these listings to confirm they are correct. It is possible, but time-consuming, to get a website to change an incorrect listing. I know—I've worked with several hundred authors and have seen every possible type of mistake made on bookselling websites.

Maximize your Amazon listing with an Author Page. You can, and should, have your book listed on Amazon before the date the book will be shipped; it's another way people can preorder it.

You need to write a basic press release about your book. Once you have your first press release, it can then be edited slightly for different media and different events. A basic press release should be no longer than one page. Make sure you add anything that a reporter might find particularly interesting, namely, a "hook" to hang a feature story on. Is the book set in the local area? Does it discuss a local historic building or event? Are there other unique touches can you think of? Also, include your contact information and paragraphs about you, your book, and coming events such as a book signing or workshop.

Send Out Review Copies

I know you want to start making money on your book right away, but the first 50 or so copies of your book are going to be given away, not sold. Look over the media list you created and decide to whom you should send a full media kit, to whom you will send a copy of the book for review, and who just needs a simple press release.

You may decide to send the editor of your local newspaper a review copy as well as a complete press kit. Regional and national media will probably need only the press kit. Book reviewers should definitely receive a copy of the book—they can't review it if they haven't read it.

This is another way in which e-books are useful. Some reviewers only want to read an e-book, either .mobi or .epub. Make sure you have both available on your computer so you can email them to reviewers who request the book in one of these formats.

Host an Event or Three

Book signings, book launch parties, seminars, and workshops—virtual or in-person. You should use them all to promote your book in the first few months after it is published. You have just accomplished something fantastic so celebrate. Some of these, such as an in-person launch party, can be by invitation only—everyone's budget is limited, after all.

You may also want to limit the number of people invited to a Zoom event. Once you have more than a screen full of people, it is just too hard to connect. You have to keep switching back and forth to different screens to see everyone, and the people really can't interact with you or each other.

Spring for the paid Zoom subscription. It's not that expensive; it gives you several benefits, most important being that you won't be automatically cut off at 40 minutes. And you are going to be using Zoom a lot to promote your book.

Being invitation-only doesn't mean you should only invite family and close friends. Invite business colleagues, referral partners, and, of course, anyone who helped you with your book such as the editor or graphic artist. Plan for book sales; designate someone to take the money and hand out the book while you as the author act as host. Network at the event, and give a short speech or reading from your book. Even if the event is private, invite the press, and send a follow-up press release and photos of the event to local media.

If you are hosting a public event such as a book signing, a seminar, or a workshop, make sure you send out as many flyers, press releases, email invitations, or other types of advertising as you can to attract a large crowd.

Event Follow-Up

The great thing about an event is you never know who you will meet—even if, or especially if, it is your own event and you have set the guest list. After all, everyone who attends your book signing or launch party presumably has come to meet you. You may not have a chance to spend as much time as you would like with every guest so have a guest book at the event to make sure you get the names and contact information for everyone who attends.

Follow up with written notes thanking everyone who helped make your event a success. Send a note or email to anyone you would like to get to know better, and, if appropriate, set up an appointment. If you are a nonfiction writer, this may be a straightforward business meeting. For the fiction writer, the goals may be less clear. But again, you never know who you'll meet and how you can help each other along the way.

Don't forget to post some photos of the event on your Facebook page, your website, and other social media, and tag the photos with the names of the people in them. People love to look at pictures of themselves and their friends. It is one more way to bring people to your website and keep you and your book in front of your audience.

Radio, Podcast, and Television Interviews

Radio and podcast hosts love to interview authors. There are literally thousands of shows on the air and online, and many run two to three hours, five nights a week—that's a lot of airtime to fill. Just as with book reviewers, you can find radio shows and podcasts to fit almost any niche market you can think of, and it is often the best way for beginners on the speaking circuit to gain name recognition outside their local area. One of the beauties of podcasts is you can be interviewed by someone anywhere in the world while sitting cozily at home. I've done several interviews with California radio stations and a podcast based out of Canada. Now that I'm a "veteran," it always amuses me when I listen to other interviews to imagine the interviewee sitting at home in his or her pajamas while sounding terribly professional on air.

A few months before you launch your book, do some research on any podcasts and radio shows related to your topic, and begin to send out query letters asking to be a guest on the show. Television can be more difficult to break into. There are fewer television stations with less time devoted to talk shows. However, just because it's difficult doesn't mean you shouldn't try. Do more research before you get started. Find out who on the staff actually chooses the guests, and direct your query to that person.

Sometimes you get lucky, and the book you have just written is on a topic that hits the news. For example, a book on airline safety that hits the press a few weeks before a major air disaster, or a biography of a celebrity who gets arrested/divorced/dies. It sounds macabre, but let's face it: Breaking news is often about the less-than-pleasant events in life. If a book you have written relates to a current news event, use it. Call your local television station and let them know you have information to share.

Another good resource to use is called HARO at www.HelpaReporter.com. Thousands of journalists working for newspapers, television, radio, and internet sites use HARO to find information and sources for their stories.

When you sign up for HARO, emails describing the stories reporters are working on arrive a few times a day. The secret is to learn to quickly scan the entries for reporters who are working on stories in your niche. Then reply to the email with a short summary of how you can help the reporter. Do not give up if you do not find anything in the first few weeks, and make sure you follow the rules of etiquette for the website.

Using Podcasts to Sell Books

With a little planning, a podcast can be an excellent way to connect with new potential readers, particularly if you do some planning ahead of time. Before you are scheduled to speak on any podcast or at any other event, set up a page on your website where listeners can download a special link for a free first chapter of your book.

During the podcast make sure to tell your listeners about the link. Repeat it several times if possible, and always repeat it at the end of the podcast. At the end of the free, downloadable chapter that you are giving away, be sure to include a link to purchase the book along with a call to action asking for a review. Even if the person doesn't purchase the book, he or she may just leave that review, and that is still a win for you.

I've given you a lot to think about and to do in this chapter. I know it can feel overwhelming. It doesn't have to be done all at one time. Break it down into monthly bites. What will you do the first month after your book has launched? What will you do the second month?

Looking at your marketing in small, reasonable pieces will make it that much easier.

Exercise 6
Your Call to Action

No matter what you do to market your book, make sure you include a call to action asking for a *purchase and for reviews* everywhere you mention your book.

1. On your website
2. On your Facebook page and other social media
3. At the end of your book, particularly the digital version
4. On any free worksheets or PDFs you send out
5. If you send a free first chapter of the book

Chapter 8
Amazon

Amazon is one of the greatest things to happen to writers since Gutenberg invented the printing press. Yes, I really mean that. I know many authors and publishers love to bash Amazon—I've spent my share of time bashing it myself. But Jeff Bezos, the founder of Amazon, has almost single-handedly changed the way the world buys books—and everything else.

Yes, Amazon rules the market, and it is always more fun to root for the underdog. Yes, Amazon takes a big chunk of your profit. Without it, though, you would not have any sales to profit from. Yes, Amazon is complex, but that's because it's offering so many ways for you to connect with your readers. And yes, Amazon has reconfigured the way it pays for "pages read" so that authors are making even less money. But until something better comes along, Amazon is your best shot at successful self-publishing so learn to use it.

We'll start with the basics. Much of this is also covered in my book *Self-Publishing: You Can Do This!* But it never hurts to go over it again.

Uploading Your Book

To upload your book, first go to KDP.Amazon.com. KDP stands for Kindle Direct Publishing, the publishing arm that Amazon uses for both e-books and paper books. In the past Amazon had a website for publishing paper books called Create Space. When you first click on the "bookshelf" section of KDP, you'll see a note about Create Space. If you have never uploaded a book before, don't let it confuse you. Just move on!

At Amazon you can use one email and login for everything—from buying anything such as toilet paper and auto parts to uploading your own books to sell, or setting up your Author Central page.

When setting up your first book, it will be easiest if you gather a few things first. The first time you set up a book you will have to fill out some forms including tax information and information about your checking account so Amazon can send you royalties. Have your Social Security number, your bank routing number, and bank account number handy. You must fill this section out before you can submit a book for publishing so you might as well get it over with and just do it first.

Next, know where on your computer you have:

1. The formatted Word document of your complete e-book manuscript
2. A formatted PDF for your paper book
3. A .jpeg of your book's front cover
4. The template for the complete cover (front, back, and spine)
5. A short description of your book to attract readers
6. Your bio
7. Seven keywords to describe your book
8. Your ISBN
9. The price for your book
10. An idea on the genre categories where you will list your book

Follow the steps on KDP and upload your book. Plan on spending about an hour the first time you do this. If you have never uploaded a book before, you will be surprised at the number of categories and subcategories there are for book genres. Take some time to explore them thoroughly. You want to make the best choices possible for your book.

You will be asked to set a price for your book. Book pricing is very important, and I hope you have already done your research and have a price in mind based on other books in your genre. However, if your book is so many pages that the price you have chosen is not economical, KDP will automatically increase your price during setup.

Once you have uploaded your files, KDP will either approve

them or let you know by email if there is a problem. Your e-book preorder will appear on Amazon within hours of setup.

For paper books, you can choose to receive a printed proof for a minor fee. I suggest you do this. You will see things differently with the physical version than you will with the online PDF. Once you have looked the paper version over, made any necessary changes, and given final approval, your paper book appears on Amazon for sale, and you are a published author!

"Look Inside the Book" Program

You can do several things to maximize your listing on Amazon. How many times have you stood in a bookstore and thumbed through a book before deciding whether or not to buy it? The "Look Inside the Book" feature is offered free on Amazon. "Look Inside" is one of the most fun features for Amazon shoppers because it allows them to virtually thumb through the Contents and several pages of the book before choosing whether to buy it. It makes the online shopping experience much closer to going to a bookstore and gives the reader an easy way to sample the product before buying. If you are uploading both an e-book and a paper book, it should appear automatically on your listing. I have noticed, however, that books uploaded only as paper books often do not automatically have this feature on their listing page. To sign up, go to www.amazon.com/sitb to read the guidelines and learn more about the program.

Author Profile Page

Once you have set up your book, you can begin to add to your Author Profile. Start with a short bio and a photo of yourself. You can also add a caption under the photo. It should say something more than just your name. Make sure to include the title of your latest book and your website's URL.

Also, check that all of your books are listed correctly. Amazon is huge, and it is easy for mistakes to be made, particularly if, like me, you have a common name. There are dozens of Karen Millers out there, and I've found that even using a middle name doesn't always stop the confusion. Check your Author Page often to make sure that all of the books you have written—and only the books you have written—are listed on the page.

Change and update your Author Profile page quarterly; add new features and information to make it more interesting to the reader. Put up a new photo of yourself. Change out your author bio. Tell people about events where you will be. If you have written a new book, make sure it has been added to the page. Nine times out of 10 it will happen automatically, but don't be that 10th person whose new book never gets listed. It can affect your sales.

Becoming an Amazon Best Seller

Every writer dreams of being a best-selling author, and Amazon is in the business of making that dream come true—in theory, if not in reality.

One technique, which to a certain extent applies to the 100 Review Book Launch plan, that works is to have as many people as possible buy the book on the first day it becomes available.

Depending on the category your book is listed in, and the number of people you have contacted who will actually follow through and buy your book at the right time, this can work. But it is a one-day technique; if you have no follow-up, it will be the only day that you have sales.

Marketing is not a one and done process. Yes, you can do a large, successful campaign to get your book to the top of your category for a day or maybe even two days if you are in a small niche genre. But without doing additional promotions to find more readers, you will quickly fall from the top of the list into obscurity. Yes, you can put "Amazon Best Seller" in your bio for the rest of your life; if that is your only goal, go for it. As a marketing strategy, though, it will not bring you long-term sales.

When you list your book on Amazon, you have the opportunity to choose the categories where it will appear. Choose carefully and appropriately. It is more important to be listed in the best category for potential customers to find your book than it is to be listed in a tiny category so you can attempt to become an Amazon best seller.

Let's take a quick look at how the Amazon ranking system works. If you've bought a book on Amazon in the past, you may have noticed the Amazon ranking on a book's detail page. We'll use a frequently purchased book, Strunk and White's *The Elements of Style,* as our example. On the day I consulted it, this book had an Amazon ranking of 451. That ranking is calculated per hour using Amazon's proprietary algorithm, which compares sales of that book to all other books sold on the site within that hour window. What does that mean for the book's ranking? In all honesty, not much; the only thing you really know is that in that hour, *The Elements of Style* was in 451st place for number of sales *in its category.*

Instead of creating a strategy to place your book at the top of the best seller list for one day, develop a long-term marketing plan to slowly and steadily increase your rankings and sales over time.

Reviews

When readers are choosing a book on Amazon, particularly one from an author they are unfamiliar with, they are likely to be influenced by other peoples' opinions and reviews. As I mentioned earlier, studies show that 90 percent of internet shoppers read online reviews, and 84 percent trust those online reviews as much as they trust a personal recommendation. Having reviews on your book page will increase the likelihood that it will be purchased. Use the 100 Review Book Launch techniques to get as many reviews as possible in the first two months when your book is available for sale. More reviews will make it easier for you to sign up for a variety of e-book promotions over the next few months. We'll talk about these promotions in a later chapter.

Do not wait for your friends and relatives to decide to review your book. If they are not authors themselves, they do not know the importance of placing a review on Amazon. You will have to ask. You will have to twist arms. You will have to help them write reviews. One of the most common questions I hear from authors is, "How can I get my friends to review my book?"

First, when posting on Facebook about your book, always ask your friends to post a review. Next, pick a few close friends and ask politely, but very pointedly, for them to purchase the book and review it. The reviewer must have an Amazon account and have purchased items on Amazon to leave a review. (Yes, there are a few people left in the country who don't have Amazon accounts.) I recently asked a friend to review a book; it turns out she has never purchased anything on Amazon. Here's the email she got from Amazon.

"To submit reviews, customers must make a minimum amount of valid debit or credit card purchases. Prime subscriptions and promotional discounts don't qualify towards the purchase minimum."

Amazon does place the phrase "Verified Purchaser" next to reviews from Amazon purchasers. If you have an e-book, ask your friends to spend $2.99 and purchase your book as an e-book to help ensure their review will be used.

Now comes the hard part: actually getting your friends and loved ones to sign into Amazon and post a review. After you have asked nicely once or twice, it's time for strong-arm tactics. Polite strong-arm tactics, of course.

Many people have a strange fear of posting a review. Some people worry it will make them more open to hacking and other internet privacy violations. If your friend expresses these concerns, move on. No amount of reasonable logic from you will change their minds. And if they do get hacked sometime in the next 10 years, they'll blame you. Find someone else to review your book.

If someone has told you they will review your book but has not done so, I suggest this remedy. Invite them to your home or out to dinner. Make sure you have a computer or smartphone with you. Hand them your electronic device. Ask them to sign into their own Amazon page and walk them through the process.

Yes, I'm serious. It works. I've done it.

Amazon Review Myths

I constantly have authors telling me theories they have heard about why certain reviews are taken down by Amazon. I see as many examples of reviews that stay up with these problems as I do reviews taken down. Amazon seems to be quite arbitrary in how reviews are listed. Here are a few things that can cause a review to be deleted by Amazon.

1. **Nonverified purchase.** If a review has "Verified Purchase" next to it, you know the reviewer purchased the book—and presumably read it. I've heard of reviews that were not

verified being taken down by Amazon, but I know of reviews used by Amazon that are not verified. Asking your reviewer to purchase an e-book (I suggest e-books because they are less expensive) on Amazon increases the chances it will be posted.

2. **Reviews by relatives.** I often hear people say Amazon will delete reviews by relatives. I know of at least one review that was posted a few years ago and is still up that starts with the words: "proud husband of the author." The question is how can Amazon know who you are related to? If your last name is uncommon, that might be a reason. In my case, it hasn't been a problem.

3. **Connection to the author.** If Amazon decides you have a "business connection" to an author, Amazon will not allow you to review that book. For example, I cannot review books by authors I publish.

The best suggestion I have is don't worry too much about it—as long as you are being honest about the reviews you are seeking. Do NOT try to game the system. It is not worth it if you are caught. Do ask everyone you know to write a review. This way if one or two are taken down, you will still have plenty of reviews.

There are a couple of big "dont's" in obtaining reviews. ***Do NOT pay someone for an Amazon review. Do not trade reviews.*** I think the problem with paying someone is obvious. Trading reviews with other authors, however, needs some explanation. Many people join author groups and websites to gain readers and reviews for their books. There is nothing wrong with this. However, when you say, "If you review my book, I'll review yours," things can get very tricky. What if you don't like the other author's book? What if they don't like yours?

You *can* give away your books and ask for "a fair and honest review." This approach gives the reviewer the option to click less than five stars or give a less than complimentary statement about your book.

Let me make my policies on reviews clear.
• When asking good friends or relatives for reviews, be politely assertive. Do everything possible to make them sit down and actually review the book.
• When asking strangers and other authors for reviews, be careful you do not put yourself in a situation in which you

must give another author a dishonest review.

Searching for Reviewers

There is something about seeing one or two lonely reviews at the bottom of a book's Amazon listing that is just sad. And it reduces your credibility considerably. If you have used the 100 Review Book Launch plan, exhausted yourself twisting your friends' arms, and have posted your book on Goodreads, there are other ways to find reviewers for your book.

There are many Facebook groups out there—some closed, some open—that focus on connecting authors with reviewers. To connect with these groups use the Facebook search tool to look for "author reviewers" and "book lovers" groups. There are many different groups available, with a variety of focuses and rules; don't just pick the first one you find. Check out several and see which ones mesh best with your interests and needs.

Another possibility is YourNewBooks.com. This website has a "Read & Review Program." You pay to advertise to a large group of people who are interested in reviewing your genre. The site explains it this way:

With the Read & Review Program, you are not buying reviews. Buying reviews would be against Amazon's Terms of Services. However, you are purchasing:

Access to new readers and hopefully a few new fans!

Advertising space on our site and in our newsletter for your R&R book

A program that encourages our readers to leave an honest review after reading your book

YourNewBooks.com readers do not receive any compensation, other than the free eBook.

No matter which method you choose, getting reviews is not just a marketing first step but a continuing step. As you receive more reviews from people you don't know, you are more likely to get a bad review. Don't let this stop you. Don't let it bother you. Not everyone will love your work. But if you have a lot of good reviews, one bad one will have less effect on your ranking. And it will have less effect on your potential readers as well.

Exercise 7
Pricing Your Book

There is a little bit of science and a little bit of art in finding the right price for your book. It is difficult to sell a fiction book for more than $9.99 unless you are a well-known author.

Paper books
1. General nonfiction books such as self-help, memoir, or biography will usually sell for about $12.99 to $14.99. They may sell for more if they are particularly long.
2. Technical books by lawyers, doctors, financial advisors, and others who are considered to have a lot of specialized knowledge can sell their books for higher prices. Depending on the profession and the size of the book, they can sell for $19.99 on up.

E-books
1. Price most e-books at $3.99 or $4.99.
2. Be prepared to run periodic 99-cent and free book promotions.
3. Technical books can be sold at higher prices; $9.99 and $14.99 are popular e-book prices.

Chapter 9
Getting Reviews

While Amazon customer reviews are important, there are also many other aspects of getting reviews for your book. Traditional book reviews, those long, thoughtful, critical *The New York Times*-style reviews, and "blurbs"—short reviews or testimonials at the front of your book or on the cover—are also excellent ways to bring your book to the attention of a new audience.

The more people who review your book, the greater exposure it has to new and different people who are potential customers. Do not underestimate the power of these types of reviews. Think of them as a form of peer pressure. We are all influenced by what other people are wearing, buying, or talking about.

I know a lot of you just turned your noses up at that idea. "I don't care what other people think. I make my own decisions," you said to yourself. Think again. Do you check *Consumer Reports* before purchasing a large ticket item? Do you ask your friends for recommendations when you need to find a doctor, dentist, or car mechanic? Have you ever bought a book because you heard other people talking about it? Yes, you are influenced by what other people think. That's why getting your book reviewed is an important technique in selling it.

Prepublication Reviews

It's a great idea to have some reviews or testimonials before you publish your book. Who should you ask to give you these reviews? The most influential people you know ***who are in your*** *field*. A review from an unknown person is much less impressive in this case than a review from a person with some credentials. A review from someone whose expertise is totally unrelated to your topic, particularly if your book is technical in nature, is also fairly meaningless.

Once again, think about your target market. Who is considered a leader in their eyes? If you are writing a book about health care, get a leading doctor to write the review. If you are writing a book with a regional influence such as a history of your town or area, ask the head of a local museum to write a review. You get the idea.

These blurbs can be used on the back cover of the book or just before or just after the title page. You should also place them on your website.

Don't be shy. Think of the most well-known people in your field and approach them. If you aren't personally acquainted with them, try to get an introduction through a mutual acquaintance. If you are in the same field, you may want to reference a trade organization or other connection that you share. What's the worst that can happen? The person will say no to you, and you will move on to the next one on your list.

Don't Be Afraid—Just Ask

I've spent more hours coaxing writers into asking their heroes for reviews than I can count. "He won't review my book. He's so much more important than I am." That's the line I most often hear. It's amazing, though, how many times a simple email asking for a review is answered in the positive.

When you ask, however, make sure you give a deadline date. Even the most well-intentioned person will put things off, particularly, it seems, when writing a review. I'm not sure why, but even professional writers may hate to write reviews. So make it clear that (1) you only expect a few sentences, and (2) you must have it by a specific date, which will make it much more likely that your request will be granted—and the review completed and returned to you. Don't forget to send a thank-you note when you receive the review, and make sure you send the reviewer a complimentary copy of the book when it is published.

Sometimes the reviewer will ask you to send something

specific, three chapters for instance, or a paper copy (rather than emailing a document). If no special requests are made, the easiest thing is to email a clean, final draft of your book in PDF form. Make sure it is the most complete and error-free copy possible. Have the manuscript checked by a proofreader before you send it to someone to review. A manuscript filled with typos and mistakes won't make a great impression. If for some reason (usually time constraints) you cannot send the final draft, make that clear to the reviewer—as well as the fact that you do plan to have it proofread before it is published.

To ask for a review, send an email explaining exactly what you want—a two- or three-sentence review of the book is just fine. In fact, anything over one paragraph can be difficult to place in your book. It is also polite to add a link to a reviewer's website or reference the person's work when you print the review.

For example, identify the author of the review as "Antoinette Brown, author of *The Poor Man's Guide to Great Wines,* www.poormanswine.biz."

Amazon Reviews

We discussed Amazon reviews previously, but they are important enough to mention again. This is when you can call on your friends and relatives. Ask everyone you know who reads your book to add a review on Amazon. Good reviews matter. People do read them, they do influence their decision to buy, and gaining at least 10 reviews makes you eligible to advertise on a wider variety of e-book marketing sites.

Do not just count on random reviews from unknown people who have purchased your book on Amazon. You can send your book and request reviews from potential reviewers on Amazon's Top Reviewers list: http://www.amazon.com/review/top-reviewers.

Once again, take the time to read about the reviewers. Look for people who review books that are similar to yours. If you are writing historical fiction, don't send your book to a reviewer who only reviews mysteries. If you are writing a how-to craft book, don't target the business book reviewer. While this seems obvious, it is not always easy to find this information out. Make sure you read everything thoroughly on the reviewer's site so that you do not make embarrassing mistakes. Of course, you have no control over what a reviewer says. You may get a bad review; it's just one of the chances you take as an author.

Give and You Shall Receive

Take the time to review other people's books. Why? Well, first, it is just a thoughtful thing for you to do. If you like the book, write about it and let other people know why it is good. Second, it is one more way to get your name out there.

Put reviews on Amazon. Write reviews on blogs and other public forums where you can add the title of your book and a URL to your website in your signature. I've noticed that savvy authors often review other authors' books. Consider it one more marketing tool.

Send Out Review Copies of Your Book

As soon as you receive copies of your book, send them to reviewers. Figure that at least the first 50 books you receive will be given away, not sold. Yes, this hurts. You have just spent a lot of money publishing your book, and you want to start earning it back right away. Remember this marketing rule: Every copy of your book that you give away results in approximately 10 additional sales. Send out review copies as soon as possible. A new book is news; a six-month-old book is not.

Where to Find Reviewers

Hundreds of blogs and websites on the internet focus just on book reviews. Some major newspapers and magazines still have book review columns, and there are also radio shows and podcasts—on the air and on the internet—devoted to books. Once again, figure out who your tribe reads and listens to. Are there blogs aimed at your target audience? Send those bloggers a free copy of your book.

Some authors now distribute complimentary review copies of their books through at least two online sites, Goodreads.com and LibraryThing.com. You can ask—not demand—that reviewers who receive a copy of the book post a review at Amazon as well as on the site where they received the book. Some reviewers will do this, others will not.

Journal Reviews

There are also book review journals that are read by librarians and bookstore managers. These people make a lot of their purchasing decisions based on reviews in these journals. Unless you have a major publisher behind you, however, it can be difficult to get your book reviewed in these journals unless you pay for a review. While it is certainly a legitimate marketing technique, it is difficult to accomplish for the average author. If your time is unlimited, it could pay off. But if you are juggling a full-time career and a family, this should not make your top 10 list of marketing strategies to try.

Paid Reviews

There are probably more differing opinions on the value of the paid review than there are journals that place them. *Publishers Weekly* now publishes paid reviews as well as unpaid reviews. For those unfamiliar with this publication, it is probably the oldest news magazine aimed at the publishing trade. Its target market is publishers, librarians, booksellers, and literary agents.

Another standard of the publishing business, *Kirkus*, is one of the biggest reviewers for independent authors. Midwest Book Reviews offers both paid and unpaid options.

BlueInk Reviews (www.blueinkreviews.com) uses an "extensive roster of well-vetted and thoughtful critics—all with proven track records in mainstream publishing" to review books. They have paid and unpaid options. Their paid reviews are expensive—and are noted as such—but they do have greater traction with libraries.

BookLife (www.booklife.com) is the arm of *Publishers Weekly* that focuses on independent authors and small presses. It has both paid review options and advertising options. Its advertising rates are quite reasonable for the size of its audience.

Paid reviews may have less value than unpaid reviews, but they do still have value. If you are a first-time author, a paid review may be your best chance to get in front of buyers for libraries, bookstores, and other retail outlets. Once again, there is a downside. There is no guarantee a paid reviewer will give your book a good review. Maintaining the right to give a bad review is the only way reviewers and review journals can maintain their credibility, but it also makes this marketing technique a little bit chancy.

Dealing With Negative Reviews

Negative reviews happen. No matter how wonderful your book is, there is someone who will not like it. If they write about it, it can hurt your sales. But there is good news: One or two negative reviews among a group of positive ones will not hurt sales too badly. Reasonable people understand no one can please everyone all of the time.

It is difficult, if not impossible, to remove a negative review from the internet. Even if it is removed, you can never remove the negative impression it made in the minds of potential readers. Most blog sites do have policies against abuse and will take down reviews that are malicious or inappropriate. Amazon, for instance, requires that reviewers critique the book rather than express opinions about the author or other unrelated topics. According to its policies, it will delete a review that is "illegal, obscene, threatening, defamatory, invasive of privacy, infringing of intellectual property rights, or otherwise injurious to third parties." If you feel a review of your book falls into one of these categories, you can make a request with the Community Help department to have the review taken down at community-help@amazon.com.

Virtual Tours and Book Bloggers

There are hundreds, if not thousands of book bloggers online. They have followings. If they recommend your book, it can dramatically increase your sales. It is time-consuming to do the research for book bloggers in your genre, but it can be done.

Bloggers come and go. They may be very active for six months, a year, or even a few years, then get tired of the "job" and disappear from the blogging scene. Always make sure the bloggers you are sending something to are still active and that they review books in your field. Pick out a half dozen or more to target to make sure you get the number of reviews you want.

An additional benefit to getting your book mentioned by a book blogger is that it is an additional site where your book, and you, are mentioned online. That makes it easier for someone looking for you, or a book like yours, to find you when they search.

One excellent strategy to gain reviews as well as increased internet visibility is a virtual book tour. Just like a traditional tour, on a virtual tour the author is "a guest" on a series of book blog sites over the course of a few days or weeks.

You can set up your own virtual tour, or you can use a service that sets up your blog tour for you. I am most familiar with Bewitching Blogs Tours, but there are others out there. I Read Book Tours is another site I am less familiar with. These sites are very cost-effective, and I highly recommend them. Bewitching Blog Tours works best for fiction authors. I Read Book Tours works with a wider variety of books, including nonfiction.

Exercise 8
Where and When to Use Reviews

There are a lot of ways to use reviews.

1. You'll want to put a couple of great reviews on the back cover.
2. If you have enough of them, place some on the first page, right after the copyright page. You may need to shorten the reviews to just a sentence or two to get them to fit.
3. If the review is from someone particularly influential, you many even consider putting it on the book cover. Be careful here. If the person isn't well-known, it can detract from the cover.
4. If you do need to edit your reviews to a few sentences because you have a number of them, consider putting the full version on your website.
5. You can also use them in press releases about your book.
6. Add them to your Author Page on Amazon.

Chapter 10
More Marketing for Your E-Book

Today the least expensive way for authors to develop an audience beyond the reach of their immediate circle of friends or clients is e-book marketing.

The initial startup costs for producing a great e-book are the same as for a paper book (editing, proofreading, cover design, and formatting). If you only plan to publish as an e-book, you may not need an ISBN. Amazon will assign you an Amazon Standard Identification Number (ASIN). Smashwords and some of the other services do require an ISBN, however.

Once you get to production, the cost for an e-book is negligible, particularly compared to a paper book. There is no cost to upload the book to the various selling sites. There is no cost to print the book. There is no cost to ship the book. Best of all, there are inexpensive ways to get the word out about your book to literally thousands of readers at one time.

There are several sites on which you can upload and sell your e-book including:

- Amazon
- Barnes & Noble
- Kobo
- Smashwords
- iBooks
- Google Books

We are going to start by talking about Amazon Kindle Direct

Publishing, specifically the KDP Select program. Once you have mastered KDP, the other sites are all similar. I do suggest that if you are a first-time author, start your e-book marketing with the Kindle Select plan. Why? *Currently approximately 75 percent of all e-book sales are through Amazon Kindle.* If you want to make a name for yourself as an author, you need to increase your sales rank. Maximizing your sales on only one platform will help you to do that. The Kindle Select program easily allows you to create special promotions. Used in conjunction with other promotions, this program can greatly increase your e-book sales. Think of it as the snowball effect: Increasing e-book sales in the specific weeks when you run specials can increase your sales ranking. This gives you increased visibility on Amazon, which, in turn, increases your rankings.

To use the program you must first make sure that your e-book is not available on any other platform (only Kindle). If you have already uploaded your book to other sites, take it down. Then go to your Kindle Direct Publishing "Bookshelf" and select the "Kindle Select" option, which increases your royalties to 70 percent.

Uploading Your Book

If your book is not yet listed anywhere, go straight to www.kdp.amazon.com. If you have not used the site before, you will be directed to the account setup section. As mentioned earlier, to set up an account you will need your Social Security number, bank routing number, and bank account number. You will be required to fill out a tax interview form. *Yes, you must do this because you want Amazon to pay you royalties.* To do so, Amazon must know where to send them, and you must pay taxes on them. You will not be allowed to upload books without completing this information.

Once you fill out your tax information, click on the "Bookshelf" tab on the top left of the page. Click on "+ebook square" and fill in the information.

Now you are ready to upload your manuscript, which may take anywhere from a few minutes to an hour depending on the size of the book, the number of links it has, and your internet speed.

Once the book is uploaded, use the preview option to make sure it looks right. The program will also look for spelling mistakes. This is your last chance to make corrections. Look over the mistakes listed, make any corrections necessary, and upload again if needed. *If you plan to use the preorder feature, make sure you have made all your corrections and uploaded again before clicking "publish."* Once you have clicked "publish" with a preorder, you will not be allowed to change your manuscript before your book goes on sale.

Upload your cover. If your cover does not follow the guidelines in terms of number of pixels, you must correct the problem and upload again. Next, check the "yes" button to enroll in KDP Select, making Amazon the sole distributor of your e-book.

Now select your price. I suggest $3.99 for the average first-time author with a fiction book or a general audience nonfiction book. You will then follow the form on the website, clicking on "All Territories," the 70 percent royalty pricing, and, if you also have a paper version of your book, select "Kindle Match," which allows a person who purchases a paper version of your book to also download the e-book. You can choose free or 99 cents for your Kindle Match. I also suggest you enable book lending. Once you have done all of these things, accept the terms and conditions. Now you are almost ready to publish.

Choose the date your book will be published. You can have your book available for sale immediately, or you can choose to have it listed as a preorder for a few weeks. I suggest using the preorder option so you can begin to create buzz about your book with your friends, family, clients, and social media contacts.

Kindle Countdown Deals

The next two techniques are paid advertising. In all marketing, you should have a clear strategy. But when you are paying for advertising, you want to be even more clear in your goals and your audience.

For the first 45 days of your e-book campaign, you will concentrate on asking the people you already know to buy and review your book. Your goal is to get as many reviews as possible in this period.

After your first 45 days on Amazon you can run a one-week price promotion, dropping your price either to 99 cents or free. For your first promotion, I suggest you go with 99 cents. In the resources section of the book you will find a list of several e-book promotion sites. These sites put out daily newsletters to subscribers telling them about various books deals. The newsletter is free for subscribers but, as an author, you must pay to advertise. Prices run from about $25 to several hundred dollars, depending on the popularity of the site. Some sites increase the price for more popular genres such as mystery.

Once you have signed up for a date for your price promotion, make sure you go back to KDP and change your price for the dates you have selected. It's very easy to do.

Create a new Kindle Countdown Deal

1. Select marketplace.

Kindle Countdown Deals are configured by marketplace. You can schedule one Kindle Countdown Deal in each available marketplace during your current KDP Select term.

Marketplace: Amazon.com ‡

2. Choose when the promotion will start and end.

Kindle Countdown Deal promotions can run for up to 7 days.

Must be after July 31, 2017 (Why?)   Must be before October 24, 2017 (Why?)

Start: July 31, 2017   End:

8:00 AM ‡ PST   8:00 AM ‡ PST

3. Select the number of price increments for this promotion and the starting price. You will be able to view and edit your promotion schedule after clicking "Continue" below.

Number of price increments: 1 ‡   Starting list price: $ 0.99 ‡   Ending list price: **$2.99** (original list price)
(What's this?)   (What's this?)

On your bookshelf, look to the right of your book cover icon and click the "Promote and Advertise" icon. This will take you to a new page. Click on the yellow "Create a New Kindle Countdown Deal" button.

Make sure "Marketplace" is set to Amazon.com, not Amazon.UK. Choose the date your deal will start and the you're your deal will end. Then choose the price.

Now your first e-book promotion is set.

You cannot, however, just sit back and let it happen. Using an e-book selling site will boost your sales, but you need to help it along. Post your deal on Facebook, Twitter, and other social media sites. If you have a newsletter, send one out the week of your sale and include a link to your book. Think about all of the ways you can let people know your book is on sale for a week at 99 cents.

Of course, there are no guarantees in life, and the first promotion will rarely take you to number one in your category, unless you happen to have a very small niche market.

As with all marketing, e-book promotions work best when done several times. You can run a promotion once a quarter. The objective is to slowly, over time, watch your sales rank increase. It will be at its highest on the first day or two of a promotion. But with luck, after each promotion your rank will stay higher for longer.

Run an Amazon Ad Campaign

Amazon also offers a second type of ad campaign, which can be run more frequently than every 45 days called an Amazon Ad Campaign. If you choose your keywords and pricing carefully, this type of campaign can cost even less than the outside advertising needed to promote a Countdown Deal effectively. But be very careful. If you don't choose your setting well, it can also cost a lot

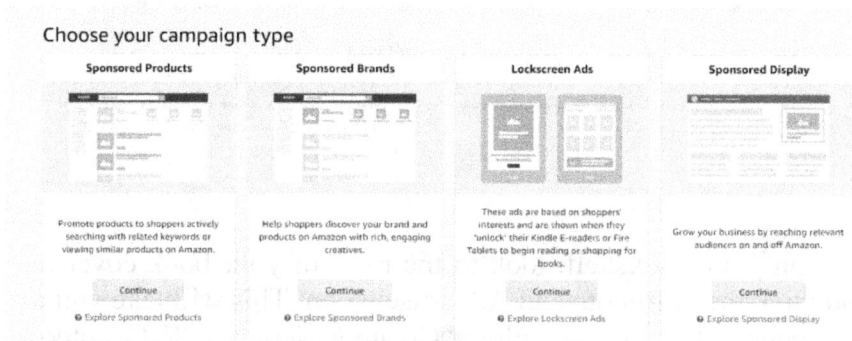

Choose your campaign type

more money.

To run an Amazon Ad Campaign, sign into your Amazon KDP Account, go to your "Bookshelf," and click on the "Promote and Advertise" button on the right side of the page. On the next page click under the "Create an Ad Campaign" box, choose your marketplace (Amazon.com), then click on the gold "Create an Ad Campaign" button.

This takes you to a new page with four boxes.

You will have to set up a "Billing and Payments" box if you have not already done so. Next, click the first box titled "Sponsored Products."

On the next page you will set the dates for your campaign—I suggest a week if this is your first time running an ad campaign. Next, set your daily budget. Again, I suggest a five-dollar top daily budget. This way you won't spend too much money on a trial run. You can then click on "Automatic Targeting" and allow Amazon to target your ads for you, or you can choose "Manual Targeting" and choose your own keywords.

Which is better? I'm not sure. I've tried it both ways and have gotten good results with both.

Scroll down and choose "Dynamic Bids—Down Only." This means that Amazon will lower the price of an ad if it considers you "less likely to make a sale." It will never raise the price of an ad.

In the "Ad Format" box, decide if you would like to create custom text for your ad or allow it to run without text. Again, first-timers may want to choose the easier route.

In the "Settings" box, give your campaign a unique name so you can keep track of how it has gone. This is very important if you run a lot of campaigns.

Next, under "Products," select the name of the book you want to advertise. Finally, set a "default bid" price (I suggest 75 cents), then click the "Launch Your Campaign" button.

Make a note of the day your campaign starts, and follow the reports and rankings for your book.

Reading Your Reports

To keep track of how many books you have sold on Amazon, check the "Reports" section of your KDP account. It can be found next to the "Bookshelf" tab on the top menu of the site.

The report page will show you how many paper books and e-books you have sold on Amazon. If you have more than one title, you can choose to look at all titles sold, or break out sales by title.

You can also check your "Kindle Edition Normalized Pages." This is an intricate formula Kindle uses to pay authors for books ordered through Amazon's Kindle Unlimited subscription service, which allows readers to purchase an unlimited number of books a month for one price.

Reading Your Ranking

How do you know what your rank on Amazon is? It's actually quite easy to figure this out. Once your book is online and for sale (e-books on preorder won't show a sales rank), click on your "Product Page" and scroll down to the "Product Details" section.

Product details

File Size: 2240 KB
Print Length: 267 pages
Simultaneous Device Usage: Unlimited
Publisher: Can't Put It Down Books; 1 edition (October 16, 2015)
Publication Date: October 16, 2015
Sold by: Amazon Digital Services LLC
Language: English
ASIN: B016SI78IE
Text-to-Speech: Enabled
X-Ray: Not Enabled
Word Wise: Enabled
Lending: Enabled
Screen Reader: Supported
Enhanced Typesetting: Enabled
Amazon Best Sellers Rank: #182,575 Paid in Kindle Store (See Top 100 Paid in Kindle Store)
   #773 in Books > Science Fiction & Fantasy > Fantasy > **Magical Realism**
   #1206 in Kindle Store > Kindle eBooks > Science Fiction & Fantasy > Fantasy > **Fairy Tales**
   #1510 in Kindle Store > Kindle eBooks > Literature & Fiction > **Mythology & Folk Tales**

Would you like to **tell us about a lower price?**

I've printed the product details for a book below.

First, you see various details about the book including the file size, publisher, ASIN, and ISBN if it has one. At the bottom of the list you will see "Amazon Best Sellers Rank," which gives you the overall rank, or how your book ranks in sales with all Kindle e-books in every category. Following are ranks in three categories. The rankings are updated daily, sometimes more than once a day, which is why keeping an eye on your rank throughout a sales promotion is important.

You can use this type of promotion whether you are with KDP Select or have chosen to publish your e-book on several sites. Each site has different rules about promotions so make sure you read everything very carefully before you start. You don't want to pay for a promotion and then find out you aren't allowed to run it the week you have scheduled.

Rinse and Repeat

There is an old marketing story, I don't know if it is true or not, but it goes like this: An advertising executive was putting together a campaign for Prell shampoo. The company wanted to increase sales. The advertising executive suggested the words "lather, rinse and repeat" be added to the label. Customers followed the instructions, began using more shampoo, and the company increased sales.

What's the point? You cannot do one e-book promotion and expect your book to become a best seller and stay at the top of the rankings. To increase sales you must "rinse and repeat."

Set realistic goals each time you plan an e-book marketing campaign; just don't get disappointed if you don't make number one on your first promotion. Continue to do e-book promotions quarterly. Mix it up a bit. Try different e-book promotion sites. Use the list in the reference section of this book, but also do some research and find others, too. Different combinations of promotions seem to work best for different authors and different genres.

Don't just depend on the promotion sites. Mention your promotion on Facebook, Twitter, and any other social media sites you use. It takes time and work to gain recognition as an author, but it can be done.

Chapter 11
Using Social Media

Social networking is the third leg of the publishing revolution that began with online bookstore sites and print-on-demand publishing. Together, these three developments have changed publishing forever, taking it out of the hands of large, corporate publishing houses and placing it squarely in the hands of authors and independent publishers.

Social media allows us to connect with people around the world and personally tell them about our books. It allows the stereotypical shy writer who is uncomfortable with the public spotlight to make connections and develop relationships without ever leaving the comfort of home. It allows us to tell the world about our latest books without spending a lot of money. Of course, it can also be confusing and overwhelming to a beginning social networker.

When we think about social media marketing, we often limit it to Facebook, Twitter, and LinkedIn, but it also includes blogging, YouTube, MeetUp, Instagram, Tumblr, Reddit, and a host of other sites aimed at specific niche markets. As with all marketing, it takes time to do social networking well; as more and more sites spring up, it is not possible to be active on all of them. The best plan is to look at which sites are the favorites of your target readers, then pick only a few of them and really work at them consistently.

Which Sites Will Work for You?

A personal Facebook page is where you share about you, but you should also consider a Facebook page for your book. If you are writing fiction or nonfiction for a general audience, Facebook is probably a site you want to concentrate on. However, it is not right for every author. If you have a professional or academic book, skip this site and spend your time on LinkedIn, a site that is more business related than Facebook.

Instagram and Pinterest are visual sites that use pictures and graphics. Both can be connected to your Facebook page. Pinterest is currently not as fashionable as Instagram but check out where your target readers are networking. If they are on Pinterest, you should be on Pinterest. If they are on Instagram, that's where you should be.

YouTube is an excellent place to post book trailers advertising your book, as well as short, informative, or instructional videos that show your expertise in your subject and as a speaker.

Twitter is a way to draw attention to posts and videos on other sites. Its short messages make it perfect for a quick "teaser headline" directing people to a longer piece of information. There are many other sites out there; if you hear about one that interests you, get on and use it for a few days to see what type of postings are made. Think about how it can help you find your target market. If your readers are there, you should be there, too.

Facebook Live

A newer part of Facebook is Facebook Live, which allows you to stream your own videos. Before beginning to stream, it is best to announce it on Facebook a few hours, or even days, in advance so that interested people can be prepared to watch. However, once you have recorded it, it stays on your Facebook page and can be accessed, and promoted, again. My first try at Facebook Live was at a weekend seminar I held several years ago, and I was impressed with the results. We streamed several workshops and had about 50 views for each at the time—that is, 50 people who saw the workshop who were not able to attend in person. But the real success came over the next few weeks, as we reposted the videos. Within the month each video had several hundred additional views.

Facebook Live is easy to do. You simply click on Facebook on your phone, then click on the "Live" button. One tip we quickly learned: You must hold your phone sideways for the picture to show in the correct access. Also, make sure your volume is on high and that you have a well-charged battery or a portable battery charger with you. That's all it takes to be live on Facebook!

Goodreads

Goodreads is a social networking site for book lovers. If you do only one thing on social media, it should be Goodreads. The first thing to do is to sign up as a reader. Get familiar with the site, fill out the information on what you are reading, join a few groups, and begin to participate in discussions.

As soon as your book is published and available online, sign into the author section and "claim" your book. Fill out some of the basic questions about your book, such as "what motivated you to write this book?" You can also sign up for a book giveaway if you have a paper book. You choose the number of books you will give away, post it on Goodreads, and people sign up for a chance to get a free book. Goodreads takes care of the details and sends you the names and addresses of the winners. I suggest you plan to give away five to 10 books. You mail the books to the winners. Sign the books and add a nice note asking the winners to review your books. Personally, I've had little success with this technique. Most of the winners of the books did not write reviews, but I do know people who have had better results.

While only a few people receive free books, the giveaway can generate interest. During a recent giveaway by a young adult author, more than 800 people signed up. The final giveaway generated two reviews on Amazon and several book sales.

Along with Goodreads, there are a couple of other lesser known social media sites for readers and authors that you might want to check out. Riffle is similar to Goodreads in style.

Squirl is an odd little app for your cellphone that allows authors to tag locations that are mentioned in their books. If a reader who has the Squirl app on their phone passes this location, their phone beeps so they can find out about books that mention that location. For example, if a reader happened to be in Salem,

Massachusetts, they might be signaled about *The House of the Seven Gables*.

Clubhouse

Clubhouse is an invitation-only, audio-chat, iPhone app launched in 2020. It is voice-based (i.e., other people on the app do not see you), and it is not based on typing messages. It advertises that people on the app "talk, listen, and learn from each other in real time." The app is divided into topics so you can join a group that is discussing only an area that you are interested in.

Blogging

Many people forget about blogging when discussing social networking, but it is a very important part of the equation for an author. Blogging is, after all, an online journal, and many writers are avid journal writers. Because of this, a blog can become a place where writers experiment and spark their creativity by getting into the habit of writing on a daily basis.

Blogging, however, has one advantage over a private journal. Bloggers can also get feedback from their readers and promote their next books by posting book excerpts, writing generally about their subject, reposting articles and other bloggers' insights on their topic, becoming known in their field, and increasing their search engine rankings.

Writing a blog is not that different from other types of writing. You want people to read your blog, just as you want them to find your book, buy it, and read it. Use Twitter to bring your followers to your blog. Not only should you be blogging on your own website, but you should also consider guest blogging or blogging on a site such as SheWrites or writing reviews on sites such as Goodreads. Find out which blogs and social networking sites your target readers frequent, and make sure you are also on those sites.

Consistency and Participation

No matter which sites you choose to use, if you aren't consistent in your posting, you won't get very far. My personal experience: I opened a Twitter account several years ago. I didn't really know why I was posting, and being a wordy writer, I had difficulty with the 140-character format. I would tweet once every few months or so, and for a couple of years my Twitter account languished with about 50 followers. Finally, I decided to really become consistent with my social networking. I got some help from an expert and really started to understand the how and why of Twitter. I began posting tweets several times a day. Guess what? My Twitter following began to increase daily. Within a few weeks I had more than 200 followers; within a few months I had more than 2,000 followers.

The secret to any social networking site is participation. If you don't check your sites regularly, it won't do you any good to be there. On LinkedIn, find discussion groups that relate to your book and participate in their discussions. Share tips and advice. Tweet daily and respond to tweets from your followers. The same is true of Pinterest, Facebook, and any other site you choose. Becoming a valued contributor increases your credibility and visibility—and encourages book sales as well.

More About Blogging

If you are an author, you should be writing daily, which means you already have material ready and waiting to post on a blog. If you don't have a blog, set up a blog page on your website. If you don't have a website, set up a blog page. WordPress is one of the most popular sites to set up a blog. Go to wordpress.com, follow the steps, and set up your blog free in minutes. It really is that easy—and as you may have noticed as you read this book, I'm not a person who is particularly good with technology. So if I say it is easy, it *really is* easy.

Here are a few blogging tips to get you started:
1. **Be consistent.** Blog at least once a week, then tweet about your blog and share it on Facebook and other social media.
2. **Use keywords.** Think of several keywords people will use when searching for your topic, and use them in your blog posts.
3. **Guest blog.** And return the favor. Research others who are blogging in related fields, and ask them for guest posts.
4. **Be patient.** It takes time to develop a following. Social media

is both the greatest thing to happen to entrepreneurs and small business owners—and as an author you are an entrepreneur—and the worst thing to happen. Social media has brought us the ability to connect with people all around the world and tell them about our products and our expertise. It can also be confusing, overwhelming, the fastest way to make a mistake, the quickest way to make an apology, and the easiest way to waste time while telling yourself you are actually being productive and "networking to promote your book."

There is always a "next big thing" in social media. It's a great way to create interest before your book is finished. Share about the process of writing. Post paragraphs and excerpts. Ask for feedback. Use social networking sites as a focus group; test out a title, versions of your cover, or ask for feedback on the development of a character. Don't be shy. These are your friends. Let them know how excited you are about the publication of your book.

But talking just to friends is not enough to turn a book into a best seller. You also need to reach people you don't know. That means starting a second Facebook page for your book. Use the book title, and make sure you include links to your website, preorder page, and other appropriate pages.

While we are talking about social networking, let's not forget Twitter. The secret to Twitter, as with all social networking sites, is to post regularly. Tweeting is all about offering excellent, relevant, and timely information about your subject. Be engaged; help people. Retweet and point people to others. Most important, posting a "buy my book" tweet three times a week will do less than no good. Tweeters HATE people who only post sales pitches. Twitter works best in concert with blogs and videos in which the author is not directly talking about a product, but rather giving advice. Tweet three to five times a day, making sure to point people to things that can help them, not just your book. As an author, no matter what subject, other authors will follow you. Growing your name means helping other people grow theirs.

That said, my experts tell me that Twitter is a lousy marketing tool for actually selling your book because many of your followers are also promoting a product. It is, however, an excellent way to increase your name recognition and build your network.

Exercise 9
What Are Your Goals?

Until you decide on your specific goals for social networking, it is difficult to develop a strategy for which sites you should be on and what you should be posting. Your goals might include:

1. Increase your professional contacts.
2. Become known as an expert.
3. Reconnect with old friends and colleagues.
4. Develop prospects for your business.
5. Demonstrate your abilities as a speaker.
6. Let people know about an event.
7. Tell people about your book and where to buy it.

These goals are very general, but they are a good starting point to help you come up with a more specific strategy.

Chapter 12
Build Your Brand

Branding is creating an image that comes immediately to mind when your name, the title of your book, the series of books, or your company name are mentioned. When the talk turns to brands a couple of companies with a great brand strategy always come up, such as Nike and Coca-Cola. Talk about branding for books, and what do you think of? Stephen King? Harry Potter? The Dummies books? Ann Rice? Some of these are authors, and others are series titles; some are fiction, and some are nonfiction. But they are all brands with international recognition.

You, too, have a brand. It may not be internationally known, or even nationally known—yet. Among your friends, your clients, and your business colleagues you have a brand. Are you known as approachable or unapproachable? Reliable or unreliable? An expert people can turn to for advice or the last person to ask? You get the picture.

If you are already in business, you are developing this brand awareness for your business as well as for yourself. Now is the time to brand both your book for its excellent writing style and great information, and yourself as an expert author.

Branding is an enormous subject, and it has many aspects to it. If you discuss branding with a graphic artist, you will hear that your business card, your website, and your book cover should all have one unified theme—the colors, fonts, the overall tone, and style should match on every web page and every piece of paper you send out. If you talk to a business coach, you will hear about how to become a great referral partner. If you talk to a presentation coach, you will hear about style of dress and your elevator speech. If you talk to someone in marketing, you will learn that you need a tagline, a great brand name, and interesting marketing copy. All of these people are correct. Your brand involves all of these things, and more.

Make sure you won't outgrow your brand. Let's say you are a lifestyle coach starting out in business. You want to focus on helping people who need to lose weight so you choose a diet-related business name like The Weight Loss Guru. After a few years you find this is too limiting. You want to talk to people who have health issues such as heart disease and diabetes and need to change the way they eat, but are focusing on nutrition, rather than weight loss. Your brand, which you've spent a lot of time, money, and energy developing, no longer fits. You need to rebrand yourself. It will be much easier and less expensive in the long run if you choose a brand that can grow right along with you.

Branding is important for fiction authors, too. Nora Roberts, for example, was already famous for her romance novels when she decided to create her futuristic mystery series, which she writes under the pen name J.D. Robb. All of the titles in her *In Death* series have the words "in death" in the title, for example, *Naked in Death* and *Brotherhood in Death*. The covers are also each stylistically the same. When you see the characteristic cover design—the name "J.D. Robb" or "in death" on the cover—you know you are getting a different type of book than one with the author name "Nora Roberts" on the cover.

What Constitutes Your Brand?

We'll start with the title. The title of your book cannot be boring or generic. It needs to be catchy, easily searched on the internet, and something in which you can obtain a URL. Search your proposed title on the internet and on Amazon. What do you come up with? Are there already similar sites and books? Or sites you don't want to be identified with? Just because there are similar titles or websites out there doesn't mean you need to change your title. Check them out. They are your competition. How do you look in comparison to them?

However, if the name you choose puts you into a group of

websites or books that have nothing to do with what you are writing about, you may want to rethink it.

The best way to create a brand is to write more than one book on your subject. Think of an appealing, brandable, nongeneric name for your series. Most first-time authors don't start out with an idea for a series. Think ahead. If you do write a second book, what can it be called? How will it relate to your first book? The title, the font, and the style of the cover are all potential elements in branding your books and branding yourself.

I've mentioned this in several other areas but let me say it once again: If you do not have a website, get one. What is the most important thing you want people to remember? If you are writing one book and never plan to write another, the website URL should be the title of the book. Do you want to use your book as a springboard for a speaking or consulting career? Your URL should be your name. Do you have a business associated with your book? Use that name as your website. Or consider all three choices. It is not really possible to buy every URL associated with you, your book, or your business, but do consider owning several URLs. They can all link back to one website.

Brand Yourself

Whether you are writing fiction or nonfiction, you are the brand. Your bio should reflect that. We tend to err in one of two ways on our biographies: Either we are too modest and embarrassed to talk about our true accomplishments, or we get too full of ourselves and throw around adjectives and phrases such as "world-class," "new and innovative approach," or "unique." These words and phrases are ultimately meaningless. Your bio should talk about you and your accomplishments in an interesting way that makes the reader want to learn more about what you have to say; in other words, it needs to be about what makes the reader want to buy your book.

You may think you are the best person to write your bio because you know yourself best, but that is often the problem—you know yourself too well. Once you have written your bio, let several people read it. See what they think you forgot to mention, or what you mention that is unimportant. Better still, get a professional writer to write your bio for you.

Social media can also help you create your brand. Don't simply make connections and friends on various social media sites, get to know the people. Write blog articles about your subject and post them on a variety of websites. Join groups on LinkedIn and actively participate. Offer advice and help to others. Make sure you are known not just as an expert, but one who is willing to share your knowledge and help others.

Another way to spread the word about you and your brand is to work with the media. The first step: When the media call, answer. I was a news reporter for more than 20 years, and one thing never changed: A source who answers the phone or returns calls promptly will be used again and again. The reverse is also true: The source who is difficult to get in touch with, who is reluctant to answer questions, or who does not return calls in a timely fashion won't be on a reporter's short list when an expert is needed. What does this have to do with branding? Getting your name out there as an expert improves your brand.

Some people have the idea that if they share their knowledge with others, it will make that knowledge less valuable, or it will in some way be used against them. This is something I've seen many times in calling sources for news stories and features.

Some people I call love to help. They want to share with others, particularly someone just starting out. They know by helping others they will help themselves. Others are afraid to talk to me. They think if someone else learns their "secrets of success," they themselves will have less success. Sharing your knowledge not only helps to increase others' awareness of your expertise, it brands you as a person who cares enough to share with others.

Finally, be approachable. An author I know attended a convention a few years ago where a number of other, better known authors held seminars and book signings. He attended several and stood in line at each to have a book autographed. Two authors, both well-known inspirational writers, had very distinct but different styles at their book signings. One quickly wrote her name in each book without looking up or speaking to the fans who had just purchased her book. The second author, who had just as many people lined up at her table, spent a few moments talking to each person who approached her and personalized each signature she wrote.

Both authors left definite impressions on my friend. But which author's books do you think he will continue to seek out and purchase, and which do you think he will ignore? People will often buy books based upon their perceptions of the author—not only her knowledge, writing style, storytelling ability, or expertise, but her personality as well. Make sure your brand is of a friendly, helpful, approachable person. It will help you sell more books.

You might not be signing books at conventions yet, but you are out there in the author world, creating an impression. One of the easiest ways to help other authors is to review their books on Amazon, Goodreads, and other appropriate websites. Giving reviews is helping yourself while helping others. Spending a few minutes to post a good review about someone else's book will only bring good things to you. It increases your searchability on the internet, it increases your reputation as an expert, and since you will list your book and your URL in your signature, it will bring you more book sales and drive traffic to your website. But more than any of these things, you will be acting as a friend.

If you read a book and you enjoy it, you will probably pick up the next book that author writes. That's what branding as an author is all about. We trust the author will continue to supply us with high quality, interesting, and informative material. Quality counts. You want your brand to stand for quality and professionalism in everything you do.

Exercise 10
What Is Your Brand Promise?

How do you want your readers to see you and your books? How are you unique? What makes you different from other authors in your genre? Your brand promise is what your readers expect when they see your name on a book.

1. Your covers should be professional and give an idea of what is inside your book.
2. Are you promising excellent information? A suspenseful read? Inspiration and help? Let your readers know what to expect from you.
3. Your genre is part of your brand. Be sure you pick the right genre for your book. People looking for fantasy don't want a thriller. Look closely at all of the genres and make good choices.
4. Deliver what you promise. If you tell your readers the second book in the series will be arriving in October, make sure it does. Nothing is worse than waiting for years for the next book in a series. If you wait too long, your original fans may have forgotten you so you will have to start all over again developing your fan base.

Chapter 13
Marketing Fiction

Many publishing experts I have spoken with agree that fiction is more difficult to market than nonfiction. There is so much more of it out there. There are so many genres and subgenres and sub-subgenres. Also, readers' opinions about fiction are much more subjective. What one reader loves, the next hates, and there is no right or wrong. It's all about what the reader likes. This chapter features some tips, particularly for fiction writers. This does not mean there aren't great tips that apply to fiction in the rest of this book—there are—but these tips are especially for you.

Let me repeat this one more time: ***The day you quit marketing your book is the day it stops selling.*** It is just as important to market fiction as it is nonfiction, yet I've often found the fiction writer is the most reluctant to put themself out there—whether from modesty or shyness or a sense that artists shouldn't be bothered with mundane details such as selling their work. Talk to any successful writer in any genre, and you will learn a large part of being an author is not about writing at all. It is about getting out there and meeting people along with setting up book readings and lectures and interviews. Yes, if you want to have the time and money to write, you have to market.

Book Festivals

While you can't get out and get a booth at a book festival during a pandemic, many of these events have moved online. Book festivals occur in every state. They range from gigantic, several day affairs—such as the Miami Book Fair International, the Virginia Festival of the Book, and the Romance Writers of America (RWA) Conference—to smaller events such as the Collingswood Book Festival in Collingswood, New Jersey. Many libraries and local bookstores also hold smaller events for local authors. The best resource I know to look for book festivals in the United States is www.bookfestival.com. Unfortunately, authors cannot have traditional booths at a virtual event. Some festivals are working on creating "virtual booths" for authors to sell their books. It is not as profitable as an in-person event, but it is one more way to get out and "meet" your fans while still respecting social distancing.

Amazon vs. Book Festivals

While, as of this writing, you can't actually attend a book festival, we will assume that in the next year or so they will be back so let's look at the pros and cons of book festivals versus promoting your book on Amazon.

The pros of event selling are:

- You keep a larger share of the profit vs. a royalty from Amazon.
- You get to meet and interact with your readers. It's a good way to develop loyal fans.
- You get to network with other authors and learn from them.

The cons of event selling are:

- You must weigh the cost of the booth with the potential for sales. The higher the booth price, the more books you need to sell in order to break even.
- Don't forget to add in the cost of gas, lunch, and possibly an overnight stay at a hotel.
- It takes time to drive to the location and a lot of energy to lug boxes of books and other items to your booth, then take them down and pack them in your car at the end of the event.
- If the event is outdoors, bad weather can ruin not only your day, but your product as well. You can't sell books that have gotten wet.
- Sales you make at events will never increase your best seller ranking.

Enter a Contest

Hundreds of contests are out there: large and small, regional and national, genre-specific and general. There are contests for self-published authors and contests for unpublished authors. Find one and enter it. If you win, it can really boost your writing career. If you don't win, some contests offer feedback from the judges. If all else fails, you've lost nothing more than your entry fee.

"What!" I hear you shouting in protest. "I have to spend money to enter a contest? What if I don't win? That's money wasted."

Yes, you do have to spend money, either on contests or on something else. I've seen the notes on various LinkedIn groups and heard the complaints from writers I know. Let me say it again: Yes, you have to spend money even if you don't know if you will earn it back. And yes, those entry fees can start to add up over the course of a year. You are in business. You cannot be in business without spending some money. For the fiction writer, entering contests is an excellent marketing tool and a legitimate marketing expense.

Reviews

While we talked a lot about reviews in previous chapters, it is worth mentioning it again here because reviews are one of the most important strategies for fiction writers to gain a following. As I mentioned in the opening paragraph of this chapter, our feelings about the fiction we read are highly subjective and extremely personal so a great review on the right website can really boost your book sales.

Create Interest for Your Book

If you don't have a website, start working on developing one today. You can also share your writing in a blog, on internet groups—dozens of them are out there—and in local writing groups. Use MeetUp to find groups in your area.

LinkedIn and Yahoo are other good ways to connect with writers. Many writers have developed a following for their work by using groups such as these to generate interest in their characters and story before it is published.

Work With Schools

Many schools bring writers in for workshops, writer-in-residence programs (even elementary schools), and readings. Sometimes the writer is paid, other schools don't have the money. There are also arts grants and state and regional programs financed by either the government or an arts council that will bring writers into schools. Search the internet for programs in your area. These are still happening today via Zoom.

Depending on the situation (whether you are talking with parents or students), you may or may not be allowed to actually sell your book directly to the students. If the school is not paying you to speak, you may be able to arrange for them to purchase enough copies of the book for each of the students that you speak with, or a few copies for the school library. If you are talking about classroom sets, schools do expect a discount. School budgets are always tight but working with a school still has many advantages: You can develop a relationship and be asked to return year after year and/or you can often get some newspaper coverage for yourself and the school (make sure you check with the school before you contact the newspaper). Finally, you are giving something to the students and your community, and you have the opportunity to help young people gain an appreciation and knowledge of literature and your subject.

Give a Reading

Giving readings is one of the most important ways that fiction authors can market their work; again, it can be done through Zoom. It is the most tangible sample of your work that you can give to your readers. When you give a reading, not only do you have the opportunity to read your work, you can also answer questions about how you developed your plot and your characters, giving additional information that will make the reader more interested not only in buying the book you are reading from, but your other work—written or not yet written—as well. You can set up your own book tour by contacting libraries, arts organizations, or other groups that may be interested in your subject. For instance, historical fiction writers should contact history groups or museums. There are also cafés and coffee shops that hold open mic nights and poetry readings. Put your thinking cap on, and you can probably come up with a dozen or more sites where you can do readings.

Write Another Book

For fiction writers this is even more important than for nonfiction writers. If you are writing children's books, it is essential. Everyone loves to read a book by an author they already know. They have a sense of familiarity; they know what they are going to get. If you have created compelling characters, your readers want to know more about them. Once you get readers involved in the first book, it is much easier to get them to buy the second book, then the third book, and so on.

When promoting your second book, always mention the first book. Bring all of your books with you to your readings, and consider some type of promotion to encourage your listeners to buy more than one of your books.

Develop Add-On Products

Games, toys, CDs, t-shirts, mousepads, iPad cases—the list is endless. If you're a fiction writer, you've got a great imagination. What add-on products can be offered with your book? It's easy if you are a children's writer. Toys or dolls are a natural. Computer games are obvious for the fantasy writer. Add-ons can work for any genre. To spark your imagination, go to author Karen Marie Moning's website www.KarenMarieMoning.com and check out her "shop" page. There are dozens of ideas for merchandise branded with references to her Fever series.

Brand Yourself and Your Books

Several of the tips in this chapter involve branding. Branding is all about making your name and the names of your books familiar to the public. It can be as simple as making sure the covers of your books have a similar look and feel—particularly important if you are writing a book series.

Chapter 14
Keep the Sales Going

There was a time, not too long ago, when books were seen as something ephemeral. Traditional book publishers put out a book, heavily promoted it for three to six months, and then moved on to the next book, leaving the first one to languish on bookstore sales tables and remainder bins. They were called "the backlist" and were considered terribly unimportant.

Authors, of course, have never liked this method of marketing, and as self-publishing and small, independent publishing houses have become more prominent, many have come up with a different technique. It's called "wag the long tail." This phrase means you want to find ways to keep selling your book for several years—not just several months.

So how do you do this? You keep right on marketing. Remember one of our marketing rules: The day you quit marketing your book is the day it quits selling. Well, the corollary is also true: As long as you continue to market your book, it will continue to sell.

The great news is that as more readers purchase books online, the backlist becomes more readily available. In a brick-and-mortar store there is only so much room to house product. That means that store owners must emphasize the newest books that are most likely to attract a customer. On a virtual site, a reader can browse an author's entire backlist and catch up on older books.

Always Be Closing

Salespeople know it as "ABC: Always Be Closing." Remind people that you and your book are still out there. Keep up the social networking, continue to write your blog, and book more seminars and speeches.

When your book first comes out, no one has yet read it so it may be easier to rack up sales in the first few months. Once the majority of your tribe has bought your book, you can't expect sales to maintain the same pace. That does not, however, mean you should stop promoting. There are always new people moving into your sphere of influence—people you have not met before or people who have just become interested in the subject you are writing about. You may not sell hundreds of books a month, but 10 or 15 sales a month will add to your bottom line.

Make sure your book is available on Amazon but think about other types of retailers. Is there an online specialty store catering to your target market? If your book is about a specific sport, particularly a smaller sport such as lacrosse or rowing, there are online retailers devoted specifically to them. Crafters and hobbyists of all kinds have their own websites. Fiction writers can benefit from this technique, too. There are websites devoted to romance, mystery, and science fiction, as well as other genres.

Watch the News—Calendar Tie-Ins

Is there a breaking news event that ties in with your subject matter? Don't hesitate. Put out a press release immediately and call attention to the fact that (1) you are an expert in the field and (2) you have written a book on the subject. Making contact with HARO (helpareporter.com) is an excellent way to keep on informed of breaking news as well as journalists who are working on stories about your topic.

Calendar tie-ins can also generate news. What annual events can be used to promote your book? If your book is aimed at women, it would make a great Mother's Day gift. A book about planning a wedding should have a special promotion every June. Ghost stories sell in October, and anything about Irish heritage does well around St. Patrick's Day.

What calendar events can you use to promote your book?

Don't just think of the big days, such as Christmas or Valentine's Day. There are hundreds of special days, from the well-known such as Arbor Day to National Grammar Day (bet you didn't know about that one!) you can capitalize on. Don't forget special weeks and months, such as Women's History Month and African American History Month, too. Find yours and promote your book.

Seminars and Events

Do you give speeches or hold seminars and workshops? Make sure you always have your book available to sell at any event where you are speaking. The audience is obviously interested in what you have to say so make sure they have the opportunity to take your book home with them.

Use your book as a giveaway to add value to a seminar, workshop, or other promotion. "If you sign up for my seminar now, you'll receive my book as part of the package." It's a tried-and-true marketing technique—and it works. This also works for e-books. Once you have two books available, do a free promotion on your first book, particularly if it is part of a series. You are only giving your book away for one week, and readers will get hooked on book one and immediately purchase book two. I speak from experience here—not as an author, but as a reader. I will often use a free e-book promotion to try out a new author. There are many times I'm so hooked that immediately upon finishing the first book, I go to Amazon and purchase the second one.

Two-for-One Offers and Promotions

What other products do you sell? Promote your book in conjunction with one of your other products. For example, Book A sells alone for $15. Book B sells alone for $10. If purchased separately, your customer will have spent $25. Sell the books together for $20.

Everyone wants a bargain. You'll be amazed at how many people will buy the two together. Think of the packages you see at most bookstores. You don't have to have a special box to make a two-for-one offer. An audio tape or CD and a toy that ties in with a children's book are excellent choices for a two-for-one offer. Again, this also works for e-book series. Book one, the older book, sells for $2.99. Book two, the newer book, sells for $3.99. Create a combined e-book version that sells for $5.99. The price combinations can change and increase as you add more books to your series.

Write Another Book

I mentioned this in the chapter on fiction marketing, but it goes for writers of all genres. The best way to continue selling your first book is to write a second one. Make sure when you promote your second book you always mention your first book. Bring both with you to those seminars and speaking events, and mention the first book in press releases and during interviews. Writing a second book makes your first book fresh.

Chapter 15
A Six-Month Digital Marketing Plan

In this chapter I give you a guided, six-month plan to follow. It should be worked consistently over that time for best results. I know there is a lot of information here; that's why it's a six-month plan. Don't try to do it all at once. As you become familiar with one part of the plan, go on to the next. The secret is to just keep doing something every week to market your book.

There are more than six steps; while some of them obviously come before others, there is not a specific order in which to do everything. In fact, don't feel as if you must do everything on this list. It is more important to pick two or three steps and do them consistently and well.

Step One
Ensure Your Book Has the Best Setup Possible

1. Enroll your e-book in KDP Select if it is not there already.
2. Make sure your e-book is available in all territories on KDP.
3. Check your pricing. Look at other books and e-books in your genre and compare them. Don't just compare your book to the most well-known, best-selling author in your genre; check on books by lesser known writers as well.
4. Review genre categories. Amazon has more than 7,000 categories, subcategories, and sub-subcategories. Not all of them are listed on the KDP setup page. If you see that a book similar to yours is listed in a category you do not find on the setup page, just email Amazon and ask that your book be

placed there.

5. Review keywords. Amazon allows a total of seven keywords. Other registration sites may allow fewer. When choosing keywords think about how your reader will search for your book. Readers search for broad categories, genres, or ideas. If you were a reader searching for a book like yours, what words would you type into the search engine? There is no need to repeat words in phrases, or to add plurals. Keep your character count to no more than 250.

Step Two
Prepublication Marketing

Plan your prepublication marketing strategy to tell the people you know, and those you do not know, about your upcoming book.

1. Use the Open Door Publications 100 Review Book Launch plan.
2. Utilize your existing email mailing lists to notify people about the book.
3. Work toward an initial goal of 100 Amazon reviews in the first 45 days.
4. For good friends and close family, meet with them personally to walk them through the purchase and review process. This works!
5. Consider a virtual book tour to launch your book. (see Chapter 9). You need to contact the book tour sites at least a few months before your launch date to ensure that you get the dates you want. Once your dates are assigned, follow everything your "virtual tour guide" suggests closely.

Step Three
Utilize Amazon Resources

1. Fill out a profile on Amazon Author Central. In this section you will be able to add future editorial reviews, links to your blog, update with additional books, and add events.
2. Make sure you revisit this site about every eight to 12 weeks to update it. To complete your Amazon Author Central page go to https://authorcentral.amazon.com/. Click the "Join Now"

button (yellow button on far right). Fill out your author bio on the "Author" tab and add a color photograph.

3. Next, sign up for Goodreads. Sign in and create an author profile at https://www.goodreads.com/author/program.

Step Four
Blogger Requests

At some point in the near future, you will be participating in guest blogs/podcasts/etc. This is done to more firmly establish your name as an author in hopes that it will lead to more sales. This is a daunting task, particularly when the blogger wants you to complete a lengthy questionnaire.

To prepare for blogger requests, here are some typical interview questions/blogging topics:

1. What inspired you to write this book?
2. What types of research did you do?
3. When and why did you begin writing?
4. When did you first consider yourself a writer?
5. What inspired you to write your first book?
6. Do you have a specific writing style?
7. How did you come up with the title?
8. Is there a message in your novel that you want readers to grasp?
9. Are experiences based on someone you know or events in your own life?
10. What books have influenced your life most?
11. If you had to choose, which writer would you consider a mentor?
12. What book are you reading now?
13. Are there any new authors who have captured your interest?
14. What are your current projects?

Step Five
First Amazon Promotion

Your first promotion on Amazon will help to keep the buzz about your book going once the initial sales from your book launch have died down. You can choose to do an Amazon Ad campaign or an Amazon Countdown Deal. Both are described in detail in Chapter 9.

1. For an Amazon Ad campaign, set a goal of no more than five dollars per day.
2. Follow up during and after the event to monitor sales and expenditures.
3. For an Amazon Countdown Deal, check some of the sites listed in the Resources section of this book and list your countdown deal there.
4. Monitor your sales and see which e-book sites give you the best results.

Step Six
Social Media

1. Post on Facebook, Twitter, LinkedIn, and any other social media sites you use. Be specific: Don't just ask them to purchase, ask them to purchase and review.
2. Use reviewers, bloggers, Goodreads, and other ways to get the word out.
3. DO NOT trade for reviews!!!
4. You need a consistent online presence because you are trying to establish yourself as an author, a public figure. The key with social media is consistency so do one or two really well.
5. Facebook: Be sure to have a separate author page. There will come a time when you will be thankful that you have a little bit of separation if you use Facebook for personal use.
6. Twitter: Always include hashtags. Tweets with similar themes should have the same hashtags so when clicked on the viewer is taken to a list of every post/tweet that used that hashtag.
7. Pinterest/Instagram: Users can upload, save, sort, and manage images. Instagram should be connected to your Facebook page; it can increase views of posts.
8. LinkedIn: With this social networking site for business people, you can build a professional identity online, discover professional opportunities, and get the latest news, inspiration, and insights.

Step Seven
Utilize Email Newsletters

1. Newsletters: Mailchimp is free if you are sending to 1,000 or less emails per month.
2. A newsletter format is easy to use, and you can store templates to make the creation of new editions easier.
3. Newsletter information can include interesting research into the books, character profiles, chapter snippets, appearance schedule, book suggestions, and sales promotions.

Step 8
Optimize Your Facebook Author Page
to Sell Books

Facebook remains one of the most popular social media platforms, and if you are going to utilize it, you want to optimize your Author Page to sell your books.

To change the Author Page template:

1. Click on "Settings" in the top right hand corner of the Author Page screen.
2. Click on "Edit Page," then under "Templates," click the "Edit" button.
3. Choose the "Shopping" template, then select "View Details," and finally "Apply Template."
4. Once the template has been applied, turn off "Default Tabs" (the tab to do so will appear underneath).
5. Click and drag the "Shop" tab to the first position.
6. Click and drag the "Events" tab to the second position.
7. Click and drag the "Author App" to the third position. If you don't have an Author App yet, follow the directions below to get it:
8. In the search bar on your Facebook Home page, enter "Author Marketing App" and hit enter.
   a. Click on "Use Now," and then "Let's Get Started."
   b. From the dropdown menu, select the page you want to apply the app to, and then click on "Add App."
   c. It takes a minute, but the "Author" tab should be

visible. Once it is, follow the instructions given in number 7 above.

9. From your Author Page, click on "Shop" in the left column.

10. A pop-up screen will appear asking you to agree to the Seller's Terms and Policies.

11. Then another screen will appear asking you to choose a checkout method. Select "Checkout on Another Website."

12. Choose the currency you want your prices to appear in. The US dollar is the default setting.

13. When done, click "Save."

14. Add your product (book) title.

15. Now you have to add products (books) to your store.

16. To add a product, you will need an image that is square with a resolution of 1024 x 1024 pixels. To create this go to canva.com and create a social media image. This choice is 1024 x 1024 pixels. Once you choose a background, upload the image of your book cover. Add it to the background. Once it is to your liking, save it to your computer. You will need it for the next step.

17. Go to your Author Page again and click on the "Shop" tab, and then on "Add Products."

18. Fill out the form with the book title, price, description, and URL.

19. Search for the image you have created and apply it to this product page.

20. There are two buttons on the bottom of this product page: "Feature This Product" and "Share This Product on Your Page."

21. Featured products appear larger and are the first thing a viewer sees. This should be reserved for your best-selling item or your newest book. For this one, both buttons should be clicked on.

22. The other button, "Share This Product on Your Page" should be clicked for every other product.
    a. Set Your Button.
    b. You should have a blue button that says "Shop Now" at the top of your Author Page. To change the message on this button, hover over the button until a window appears. Select "Edit" button.

c. If your purpose is to direct your customers to your Amazon purchasing page, then you need to make sure that that web address appears in the box. A pop-up box will ask what you want it to say. There are several choices. Choose "Shop Now."

d. Occasionally, you may want to change this action button. An example would be if you are pushing for new people to sign up for your newsletter. If this is the case, clicking on the button wouldn't take the interested people to where they would sign up for the newsletter so the web address would need to be changed, and the call to action message would also need to be changed to "Sign Up."

A Final Thought

This book is by no means the ultimate word in marketing your book. There are always new things to learn and new techniques to try. The perfect strategy for one author may fall flat for another. I've seen sales strategies come and go. They work great for several months or even several years, then just stop working.

Keep looking for new techniques. Watch videos, read books, and learn new things. Just keep on telling people about your books. Develop a plan to market your book every week. If something doesn't work, don't give up; instead, try something new. That's the only secret to selling your book.

Resources

Many resources are available for writers, both in print and on the internet. It's not too surprising, I suppose, that writers love to write about writing. Here are some of my favorite resources:

The Craft of Writing

How to Write a Damn Good Novel and *How to Write a Damn Good Novel II* by James N. Frey, published by St. Martin's Press. The best books I've read on the craft of writing fiction. If you'd like to be a better fiction writer, I recommend these books. Nonfiction writers can learn a few things from them, too.

On Writing Well by William Zinsser, published by Harper Collins. An excellent book on the craft of writing.

Inventing the Truth: The Art and Craft of Memoir by William Zinsser, published by Houghton Mifflin. Memoir is its own animal, a blend of fiction and nonfiction. If you want to write a memoir, check out this book.

Finish Your Book! A Time Management Guide for Writers by Karen Hodges Miller and Lorette Pruden, published by Open Door Publications. The second book in my own Write Your Book! series. It offers a number of useful tips on finding the time, the place, and the creative energy needed to finish the book you have always wanted to write.

On Writing by Stephen King. Whether or not you are a fan of

Stephen King's books, *On Writing* is considered by many one of the best books on the craft of writing.

Style Guides

Chicago Manual of Style published by the University of Chicago Press. The final say for all issues of style in book writing.

AP Stylebook published by the Associated Press. The essential style guide for newspaper and magazine writers.

Publication Manual of the American Psychological Association published by the American Psychological Association. The most common guide for the social sciences. Use for academic writing.

AMA Manual of Style published by the American Medical Association. An online version is also available at www.amamanualofstyle.com.

The ACS Style Guide: Effective Communication of Scientific Information published by the American Chemical Society Publication. The guide for science writers.

Finding an Agent

Dozens of websites provide listings for literary agents. Two that I am most familiar with are:

Poets & Writers: www.pw.org/magazine. This magazine offers excellent information for writers, including a listing of agents in its Tools for Writers section.

Book Proposals

If you plan to look for an agent, you need a book proposal. Here are two excellent resources for nonfiction writers:

Bestselling Book Proposals: The Insider's Guide to Selling Your Work by Rick Frishman and Robyn Freedman Spizman, published by Adam's Media.

How to Write a Book Proposal by Michael Larsen, published by Writer's Digest Books.

Marketing Your Work

How to Make Real Money Selling Books Without Worrying About Returns: A Complete Guide to the Book Publishers' World of Special Sales by Brian Jud. Jud is president of Book Marketing Works, a consulting firm established to help independent publishers market their titles to non-bookstore outlets. He is host of the television series *The Book Authority* and is a regular speaker on marketing topics at the Independent Book Publishers Association (IBPA) Publishing University.

Dan Poynter's Self-Publishing Manual: How to Write, Print and Sell Your Own Book by Dan Poynter, published by Para Publishing. A nationally known expert, Poynter has more than a dozen books on writing, publishing, and marketing books.

Online Resources

When you're in the middle of writing, you don't want to be interrupted—even by something as simple as checking a spelling or looking up a definition. That's when the internet really helps. Here are some great online resources that make writing just a little easier:

www.dictionary.com. There are lots of dictionary sites out there, but I find this one of the easiest to use for a quick spelling or definition check.

www.thesaurus.com. Don't depend on the little thesaurus feature you'll find in Microsoft Word. As part of the dictionary.com site, this website makes Roget's complex book obsolete.

www.brainyquote.com. This feature of Google is one of my favorites. If you need a quote on almost any subject under the sun, you can find it here.

Book Review Sites

A number of websites are devoted to book reviews. They include both general review sites and sites devoted to specific genres.

www.goodreads.com. One of the largest online resources for readers. Its users recommend books, compare what they are reading, keep track of what they've read and would like to read, find their next favorite book, form book clubs, and more. It offers a program for authors to promote their books.

www.riffle.com. Newer than Goodreads, this site is also worth checking out.

LibraryThing is another member-based review site at http://www.librarything.com/

The Book Trap offers resources for readers at http://thebooktrap.weebly.com/readers-resource/the-midlist

The Indie View offers a very large list of book reviewers at http://www.theindieview.com/indie-reviewers/

Copyright

The US Copyright Office can be found at www.copyright.gov. You'll find a lot of useful information on copyright law. You can also register your book online or file a claim.

E-Commerce

www.payloadz.com. PayLoadz offers a secure digital goods e-commerce service to sell downloadable goods such as e-books.

www.e-junkie.com. This shopping cart service can be used for both digital and tangible goods.

www.paypal.com. Both Payloadsz and E-Junkie work well

with PayPal, a site that allows you to process credit card payments online and invoice customers.

E-Book Resources

Kindle Direct Publishing: https://kdp.amazon.com/self-publishing/ provides everything you need to know about publishing an e-book for Amazon Kindle.

Nook e-reader: www.nookpress.com is the Barnes & Nobles site for publishing books for the Nook e-reader.

www.smashwords.com. Read the "how to publish on Smashwords" section thoroughly before you begin.

www.kobo.com/writinglife. Along with allowing you to upload your book, the Kobo site also offers interesting information.

Websites

wordpress.com. A good site to host your blog or website.

GoDaddy.com. Purchase your URL, webhosting, and other services.

Amazon Resources

Maximize your listing at Amazon Author Central: https://authorcentral.amazon.com/gp/landing

For information on Amazon reviewers, go to http://www.amazon.com/review/top-reviewers

Other Resources

Barnes & Noble
To find out about working with Barnes & Noble, check out: https://www.barnesandnobleinc.com/publishers-authors/sell-your-book-at-barnes-noble/

Bowker Book Services

To obtain an ISBN and barcode and learn about other publishing services, go to: www.bowker.com

Keyword Search Sites

If you are having trouble thinking of keywords to use for your website, there are a number of free keyword generator sites available online.

www.SEOBook.com: Go to the tools section of this site for the generator

https://adwords.google.com: You can search for keywords without signing up for ads.

Grants for Writers

Poets and Writers, a magazine website with a lot more information than just grants: www.pw.org

Mid-Atlantic Arts Foundation, for writers in the mid-Atlantic States. There are similar organizations in different regions of the country and many states: www.midatlanticarts.org

Funds for Writers is a good website with a wealth of interesting information: www.fundsforwriters.com

Reposting Sites

The best way to gain more credibility from your blog posts is to repost them to other sites. Here are three popular sites, but there are dozens of others.

www.digg.com
www.shewrites.com
www.reddit.com

Tracking Sales

Here are a few sites that help you track your book sales. Some are fee-based, others are not.

Sales Rank Express: http://www.salesrankexpress.com/
Novel Rank: http://www.novelrank.com/

eBook Tracker: http://tracker.kindlenationdaily.com/
Books and Writers: http://www.booksandwriters.com/

E-Book Promotions

These sites send out daily newsletters to readers detailing e-book promotions. Costs vary. I recommend you sign up for a site and use it for a few weeks to understand how it works before you use it for a promotion. Most of the sites listed here require you to have **10 customer reviews on Amazon.**

www.Bookbub has one of the largest subscriptions, costs the most, and is the hardest on which to be accepted. But if you do get a promotion on it, you will make back your money.

www.Ereadernewstoday. A favorite of mine for romance, general fiction and nonfiction.

Some other sites that authors I know have used successfully are: www.bargainbooksy.com
www.robinreads.com
www.thefussylibrarian.com

Many other sites are out there that offer similar services. Don't just stop at this list; go online and research more. Experiment and find out which ones work the best for you. It is all about finding out which sites your potential readers are using.

Acknowledgments

If there is one thing I hope I have made obvious in the last 25 chapters, it is that it takes a village to make a book. Here is a special thanks to everyone in my own little village: Jacquelyn Pillsbury, excellent editor; Melissa Macfie, fantasy author extraordinaire and e-book marketing specialist; Jennifer Kleczynsky, who edited this book; Vivian Fransen, proofreader and Queen of the Comma; Noelle Stary, marketing expert and all-around good friend; Lisa Snyder, website specialist; and Eric Labacz, great graphic artist.

And, of course, special thanks to Sam, who always puts up with me when I'm in the middle of writing a book.

About the Author

Karen Hodges Miller is CEO and publisher at Open Door Publications, a company that specializes in helping authors navigate the world of publishing in the 21st century. The company assists both published and first-time authors with the wide variety of skills and tasks needed to successfully write, publish, and market a book.

Karen herself has written eight books, both fiction and nonfiction, as well as countless newspaper and magazine articles in her 30-year career. Prior to *How to Sell Your Book Today*, her latest book on publishing and writing is *Self-Publishing: You Can Do This!*

You can find out more about Karen Hodges Miller at OpenDoorPublications.com, on Twitter @Publisher_KHM, and LinkedIn, and at www.facebook.com/OpenDoorPublications.

If you found the information in this book useful, please leave a review at Amazon.com.

www.ingramcontent.com/pod-product-compliance
Lightning Source LLC
Chambersburg PA
CBHW060115050426
42448CB00010B/1871